Vagrant Unlocked
The Definitive Guide to Streamlining Development Workflows

Adam Jones

Contents

Preface

Welcome to *Vagrant Unlocked: The Definitive Guide to Streamlining Development Workflows*, your comprehensive companion in the journey towards mastering Vagrant as a tool for creating and managing portable, consistent development environments. In an age where software development demands agility, reliability, and efficiency, Vagrant stands out as a pivotal technology for development teams, DevOps engineers, and IT professionals who aim to enhance their workflows through standardized environments.

This book is more than just a manual; it is a detailed exploration into the myriad possibilities that Vagrant offers to streamline and transform development practices. By demystifying the intricacies of Vagrant, we aim to empower you to optimize your development pipeline, reducing setup times, minimizing environment inconsistencies, and enhancing team collaboration. This guide provides a foundational understanding of Vagrant while also delving into advanced configurations and use cases, ensuring it serves as both a beginner's entry point and an expert's reference.

Vagrant Unlocked: The Definitive Guide to Streamlining Development Workflows delves into critical topics necessary for mastering this versatile tool. We begin with the essentials—an introduction to Vagrant's core concepts and initial setup—before advancing to configuration adeptness, provisioning automation, intricate networking, and orchestrating complex multi-machine ecosystems. Furthermore, we explore sophisticated features such as utilizing snapshots to manage environment states, implementing synced folders for seamless file operations, and extending Vagrant's utility through custom plugins and scripts. Each chapter is meticulously crafted to provide depth, clarity, and practical insights, building your proficiency progressively.

Our intended audience is broad yet focused, catering to both newcomers to Vagrant and seasoned professionals seeking to refine their skills. Whether you're a developer aspiring to maintain environment consistency, a DevOps engineer focused on automating infrastructure, or an IT specialist intrigued by the power of virtualization and portability, this guide is tailored to meet your needs. With meticulous explanations, real-world scenarios, and professional strategies, this book empowers you to unlock the full potential of Vagrant in revolutionizing your development architecture.

By the conclusion of *Vagrant Unlocked: The Definitive Guide to Streamlining Development Workflows*, you will possess the capability to harness Vagrant's powerful features to establish efficient, dependable, and scalable development environments. This will lead not only to heightened productivity and efficiency but also to a more harmonious, collaborative environment for innovation and development across your teams. Engage with us as we unveil the path to an optimized development future through Vagrant.

Chapter 1

Introduction to Vagrant

Vagrant is an open-source software product for building and maintaining portable virtual software development environments. Created by HashiCorp, it provides a simple yet powerful way to manage and provision virtual machines through a single workflow. Using Vagrant, developers can easily configure reproducible and portable work environments built on top of industry-standard technology and controlled by a single consistent workflow to help maximize the productivity and flexibility of their team. This chapter aims to introduce Vagrant, explain its significance, and explore its core concepts and benefits to development teams.

1.1 What is Vagrant and Why Use It?

Vagrant is a tool that simplifies the process of managing and provisioning virtual environments for software developers. It was designed to create and configure lightweight, reproducible, and portable development environments. By automating the setup of virtual environments, Vagrant helps ensure that developers spend less time managing these environments and more time developing.

A primary feature of Vagrant is its ability to work across multiple platforms. Whether developers are using Windows, macOS, or Linux, Vagrant provides a consistent workflow to manage virtual machines (VMs). This cross-platform compatibility ensures that teams with diverse operating system preferences can work together without friction.

Vagrant utilizes a simple command-line interface (CLI) for managing its operations, making it accessible for developers with varying levels of experience. With a handful of commands, developers can initialize, configure, suspend, resume, and destroy virtual environments. This simplicity is one of the reasons many development teams prefer Vagrant over manually managing VMs.

One of the pivotal reasons to use Vagrant is its reliance on "Vagrantfiles". These files are used to describe the type and configuration of the virtual machines required for a project in a straightforward, Ruby-based syntax. The Vagrantfile provides a way to document and version-control the entire development environment specification, making it easy to share and replicate environments across teams.

In terms of provisioning, Vagrant supports automatic software installation and configuration within VMs through various provisioners like Shell scripts, Chef, Puppet, and Ansible. This feature allows developers to automate the setup process of their development environments, reducing the time to onboard new team members or to recreate existing environments.

Moreover, Vagrant integrates seamlessly with existing configuration management tools, enabling developers to reuse provisioning scripts that they might already be using. This integration fosters an ecosystem where Vagrant acts not as a replacement but as an enhancement to current workflows, allowing developers to leverage the best tools for their specific needs.

Let's discuss the advantages of using Vagrant in development environments:

- **Consistency:** By codifying the configuration of the development environment, Vagrant ensures that every member of the team works in an environment that is identical to production, reducing "works on my machine" issues and increasing the robustness of the development process.

- **Portability:** Vagrant boxes — the package format for Vagrant environments — enable developers to pack, distribute, and manage development environments in a lightweight and portable format.

- **Simplicity:** The Vagrant CLI simplifies the process of managing development environments, making it accessible to developers without deep knowledge of virtualization platforms.

- **Speed:** With Vagrant, developers can quickly spin up or tear down development environments, accelerating the setup and switch-over process between projects or branches.

- **Integration:** Vagrant's compatibility with other virtualization tools and configuration management tools allows it to fit seamlessly into existing development workflows.

In summary, Vagrant offers a unified solution to manage development environments efficiently, helping developers focus on what they do best: coding. By reducing the overhead associated with setting up and managing virtual environments, Vagrant provides a robust foundation for developing software across teams and platforms.

1.2   The Evolution of Vagrant

Vagrant's journey began with an ambitious goal: to eliminate the "works on my machine" syndrome that has plagued software development teams for decades. This vision demanded not just the creation of a new tool but the ushering in of a paradigm shift in how development environments are approached and managed.

In the early days, the process of configuring a local development environment was fraught with complexities. Developers spent hours, sometimes days, setting up their systems to mirror production environments as closely as possible. This endeavor was often complicated by differences in operating systems, software versions, and configurations. The result was a fragmented development process that hindered collaboration and productivity.

The release of Vagrant by HashiCorp in 2010 marked the beginning of a new era. The initial version introduced a simple command-line interface for managing virtual machines, but its core premise was what set it apart: it allowed developers to describe and automate the configuration of portable development environments using a single, simple text file, known as a 'Vagrantfile'.

As adoption grew, so did Vagrant's capabilities. The community around Vagrant expanded, contributing plugins, boxes, and integrations that enriched the ecosystem. Vagrant evolved from managing virtual environments in VirtualBox to supporting multiple providers, including VMware, AWS, and Docker. This flexibility meant that Vagrant could be used in a variety of contexts, from local development on a laptop to provisioning environments in the cloud.

To facilitate a more powerful provisioning process, Vagrant introduced integration with provisioning tools such as Puppet, Chef, and Ansible. This allowed developers to not only define the environment but also to specify how that environment should be configured, mirroring production setups more closely and reducing discrepancies between development and production.

Over the years, Vagrant has continued to refine its user experience and expand its feature set. The introduction of Vagrant Share was a significant milestone, enabling developers to share their local environment with colleagues or stakeholders anywhere in the world, further cementing Vagrant's role as a collaboration tool.

The evolution of Vagrant reflects a broader shift in software development towards DevOps and automation. By simplifying the creation and distribution of reproducible development environments, Vagrant has not only improved developer efficiency but has also fostered a culture of collaboration and openness. Its impact extends beyond just the technical realm, influencing how teams communicate and work together.

The evolution of Vagrant from a simple tool for managing virtual machines to a comprehensive solution for streamlining development workflows demonstrates its pivotal role in addressing the challenges of modern software development. Its journey mirrors the industry's ongoing quest for efficiency, collaboration, and consistency across development lifecycles.

1.3 Understanding   Virtualization   and Vagrant's Role

Virtualization is a technology that allows you to create an abstraction layer over physical hardware, enabling the creation and management of multiple simulated environments or virtual machines (VMs) from a single physical hardware system. Each VM can run its own operating system and applications as if running on a dedicated machine, making virtualization a cornerstone for efficient, scalable, and flexible software development.

Vagrant, on the other hand, sits at a higher abstraction level, focusing on simplifying the management of these VMs. It provides a unified workflow to automate VM provisioning, configuration, and management, ensuring development environments are easily reproducible and portable across different teams and computing environments.

The relationship between virtualization and Vagrant is symbiotic: virtualization offers the foundation for creating isolated development environments, and Vagrant leverages this foundation to streamline and simplify the creation and management of these environments. Together, they eliminate the "works on my machine" problem by standardizing development environments, making them as close to production as possible.

To connect virtualization and Vagrant effectively, it's essential to understand the roles of each component in the virtualization stack:

- **Hypervisor**: This is the layer of software that sits directly on the physical hardware or atop a host operating system. It is responsible for distributing hardware resources such as CPU, memory, and storage among the VMs. Examples include VMware's ESXi and Oracle's VirtualBox.

- **Virtual Machines (VMs)**: These are the simulated environments enabled by the hypervisor. Each VM can run its own full-fledged operating system, independent of the others and often different from the host machine's OS.

- **Vagrant**: Operating at the highest level, Vagrant interacts with the hypervisor to control the lifecycle of VMs. It does not replace the hypervisor but instead provides a layer of abstraction and automation over it, using a simple, version-controlled configuration file known as the `Vagrantfile`.

The workflow when using Vagrant typically involves the following steps, elucidated to highlight the ease with which Vagrant interacts with virtualization technologies:

1. Defining the VM's configuration in the `Vagrantfile`, including the base image to use, the network configurations, and any provisioning scripts to run.

2. Executing the `vagrant up` command, which instructs Vagrant to read the `Vagrantfile`, interact with the underlying hypervisor, and establish the defined VM.

3. Managing the lifecycle of the VM (start, stop, destroy, etc.) through Vagrant commands, abstracting the complexity of direct hypervisor interaction.

Beyond merely simplifying VM management, Vagrant integrates with provisioning tools like Ansible, Chef, and Puppet, allowing developers to automate the setup and configuration of software inside VMs. This ensures that the software environment can be recreated perfectly every time, aiding in the movement towards DevOps practices of continuous integration and deployment.

Understanding the role of virtualization within the software development lifecycle, and how Vagrant leverages virtualization to offer streamlined workflows, is essential for leveraging the full potential of Vagrant. By abstracting away the complexities of managing virtual machines, Vagrant allows developers to focus more on development and less on environment setup, leading to increased productivity and more consistent outcomes across development teams.

1.4 Core Concepts of Vagrant

In this section, we will discuss the fundamental elements that form the backbone of Vagrant. Understanding these concepts is crucial for effectively utilizing Vagrant to manage and provision virtual machines (VMs) in software development environments. The core concepts include the Vagrantfile, Boxes, Provisioning, Networking, and Synced Folders. These components work together to provide a seamless, automated, and reproducible development environment.

Vagrantfile

The Vagrantfile is a Ruby file that serves as the primary configuration file for a Vagrant project. It defines the type of machine required for a project, how to configure and provision these machines, and what kind of networking and synced folders will be used. Here is a simple example:

```
1  Vagrant.configure("2") do |config|
2    config.vm.box = "ubuntu/bionic64"
3  end
```

This code specifies that the virtual machine for this project uses an Ubuntu 18.04 LTS (Bionic Beaver) image. The Vagrantfile is integral to Vagrant's functionality, allowing for the easy replication of environments across different development setups.

Boxes

Boxes in Vagrant serve as the package format for the Vagrant environments. A box can be considered a base image used to quickly clone and create a new VM. These boxes are often OS distributions prepacked with necessary tools. Here's an example command to add a box:

```
1  vagrant box add ubuntu/bionic64
```

This command adds the Ubuntu 18.04 LTS box to your Vagrant installation, allowing it to be used in your Vagrantfiles.

Provisioning

Provisioning is the process of configuring an environment according to a defined set of parameters or instructions. Vagrant supports automated provisioning through shell scripts, Ansible, Chef, Puppet, or other provisioners. This automation ensures that the process of setting up virtual environments is repeatable and consistent across different machines and platforms. Here's an example of using a shell script for provisioning:

```
1  Vagrant.configure("2") do |config|
2    config.vm.provision "shell", inline: <<-SHELL
3      apt-get update
4      apt-get install -y apache2
5    SHELL
6  end
```

Networking

Networking in Vagrant allows configuration of how the virtual machine managed by Vagrant will access the network. It supports several modes, including port forwarding, private networks, and public networks. Here is how to configure forwarded ports:

```
1  Vagrant.configure("2") do |config|
2    config.vm.network "forwarded_port", guest: 80, host: 8080
3  end
```

This configuration forwards traffic from port 8080 on the host machine to port 80 on the guest machine, facilitating access to web servers running inside the VM from the host machine's browser.

Synced Folders

Synced folders enable the sharing of folders between the host machine and the guest VM. This feature allows for a seamless workflow where changes made to files on the host machine can be immediately reflected inside the VM. The following configuration sets up a synced folder:

```
1  Vagrant.configure("2") do |config|
2    config.vm.synced_folder "./host_folder", "/guest_folder"
3  end
```

This command synchronizes a folder named "host_folder" on the host machine with a folder named "/guest_folder" on the guest virtual machine.

Understanding these core concepts is integral for leveraging the full power and flexibility that Vagrant offers for developing and managing virtualized development environments. These components provide the foundation upon which all Vagrant functionality is built and operate cohesively to simplify the development workflow.

1.5   Vagrant vs. Other Development Environment Tools

In exploring the landscape of software development, particularly in the domain of environment configuration and management, it's essential to understand where Vagrant fits and how it contrasts with other tools that offer similar capabilities. This comparison not only highlights Vagrant's unique features but also aids in making an informed decision when choosing between tools.

Vagrant and Docker

Among the plethora of development tools, Docker emerges as a formidable counterpart to Vagrant. While Vagrant focuses on creating and managing virtual machines (VMs), Docker centers its functionality around containerization. Containers, unlike VMs, share the host system's kernel and do not require a full-blown operating system for each instance, which results in a significant reduction of overhead.

- Docker provides a lightweight alternative to the heavyweight configuration of VMs, ideal for applications that demand resource efficiency and fast startup times.

- Vagrant, on the other hand, excels in situations where a fully configured environment, mirroring a production system, is necessary. This makes it a preferred choice for development environments where the underlying OS needs to be part of the testing or development process.

Vagrant and VirtualBox

VirtualBox is another key player in the virtualization space. As an open-source virtualization product, VirtualBox serves as a foundation upon which Vagrant builds. Vagrant uses VirtualBox, among others, as a provider to create and manage VMs. The relationship between Vagrant and VirtualBox is symbiotic:

- VirtualBox offers the virtualization layer, enabling the creation of VMs on a physical machine.

- Vagrant adds a layer of configuration and management on top of VirtualBox, simplifying the workflow of provisioning and controlling VMs with simple commands.

Vagrant's ability to work with multiple providers, including VMware, AWS, and others, further extends its versatility beyond what VirtualBox alone can offer.

Vagrant and Ansible

Ansible, unlike Vagrant, is a tool designed for configuration management and application deployment. While Vagrant primarily focuses on the creation and configuration of virtual environments, Ansible emphasizes automating the software configuration within these environments or physical ones.

- Ansible uses a simple syntax written in YAML to define the configurations for applications and infrastructure, making it accessible for developers and SysOps alike.

- Vagrant encapsulates the environment setup process, allowing for the integration of configuration tools like Ansible. This means Vagrant can be used to spin up a VM, and Ansible can then configure software within that VM as per the project requirements.

This seamless integration showcases how Vagrant complements rather than competes with configuration management tools like Ansible.

Comparison Summary

To summarize, while each of these tools—Docker, VirtualBox, and Ansible—serves a distinct purpose in the development process, Vagrant uniquely positions itself as a versatile vagabond among them. It harmonizes the provisioning and management of virtual environments, leveraging the strengths of the underlying technologies.

- Docker excels in container management and is preferred for isolated environments where resource efficiency is critical.

- VirtualBox provides the virtualization technology that Vagrant utilizes for VM creation and management.

- Ansible shines in configuration management and application deployment, which Vagrant environments can seamlessly integrate with.

Understanding the distinctions and complementary nature of these tools elucidates Vagrant's role in simplifying the development environment setup, making it an indispensable tool for developers seeking efficient and reproducible development workflows.

1.6   Installation Requirements

The installation of Vagrant necessitates the prior installation of two principal components: a virtual machine provider and the Vagrant software itself. This section will delineate the system requirements and prerequisite software for installing Vagrant on various operating systems, ensuring a smooth setup process.

Virtual Machine Provider

Vagrant operates by orchestrating virtual machines (VMs) provisioned by a third-party provider. The most common providers are:

- VirtualBox
- VMware
- Hyper-V

VirtualBox, an Oracle product, is the default provider for Vagrant and is free for personal and commercial use. It supports a wide array of guest operating systems including but not limited to Linux, Windows, and MacOS.

VMware, offering both Workstation for Windows and Linux, and Fusion for MacOS, is renowned for its performance and features. Note that using VMware with Vagrant requires a separate plugin and is a commercial product.

Hyper-V is a feature in Windows 10 and Windows Server editions, requiring no additional installation for these platforms. However, its compatibility with Linux guests can be limited and may necessitate specific configuration adjustments.

System Requirements

Installing Vagrant is contingent upon the following system prerequisites:

- A 64-bit processor with at least 4GB of RAM (additional RAM may be necessary depending on the number of VMs and their memory requirements).

- At least 20GB of free disk space, though the requirement may increase based on the size and number of the Vagrant boxes.

- Administrative or root access to the system for installation purposes.

- A current version of a supported operating system: Windows 7 or higher, MacOS X 10.12 or higher, or a recent version of Linux (such as Ubuntu, CentOS, or Fedora).

Installing the Virtual Machine Provider

Before installing Vagrant, ensure that a compatible virtual machine provider—typically VirtualBox due to its no-cost and comprehensive platform support—is installed. The installation process involves:

- Downloading the latest version of the virtual machine provider from the official website.

- Following the installation instructions specific to your operating system.

- Verifying the successful installation by launching the application and, if applicable, creating a test virtual machine.

Installing Vagrant

With the necessary virtual machine provider in place, proceed with the Vagrant installation by:

- Navigating to the official Vagrant website (`https:www.vagrantup.com`) and downloading the installer for your operating system.

- Running the downloaded installer, which will guide you through the necessary steps for your platform.

- Confirming the installation by opening a terminal or command prompt window and executing the command `vagrant -v`, which should display the version of Vagrant installed.

Note: While Vagrant supports multiple virtual machine providers, simultaneous use may require additional configuration and considerations, particularly concerning default provider settings.

Upon fulfilling these requirements, your system will be equipped for Vagrant projects, allowing the creation, configuration, and management of portable virtual development environments.

1.7   Installing Vagrant

Installing Vagrant is a straightforward process, but it is crucial to follow the steps carefully to ensure a successful installation. Vagrant is supported on multiple operating systems, including Windows, macOS, and Linux. This section will provide detailed instructions for installing Vagrant on these platforms.

Pre-requisites

Before proceeding with the installation, ensure that your system meets the following requirements:

- A compatible operating system (Windows 7 or later, macOS 10.12 or later, any recent version of Linux).

- Virtualization support should be enabled in the BIOS.

- At least 4GB of RAM, though 8GB is recommended for better performance.

- Sufficient disk space for the virtual machines you plan to provision (at least 10GB free space).

- An Internet connection to download Vagrant and any necessary boxes.

Installation Steps for Windows

1. Download the latest version of Vagrant from the official website (https://www.vagrantup.com/downloads.html). Be sure to select the version that corresponds to your Windows architecture (32-bit or 64-bit).

2. Run the installer file you downloaded. During installation, you can accept the default settings.

3. After completing the installation, open a command prompt window and verify the installation by running:

```
1    vagrant --version
```

You should see the installed version of Vagrant displayed.

Installation Steps for macOS

1. Visit the Vagrant downloads page (https://www.vagrantup.com/downloads.html) and

download the .dmg file for macOS.

2. Open the downloaded file and follow the on-screen instructions to install Vagrant. This includes dragging the Vagrant icon into your Applications folder.

3. After installation, open a Terminal and confirm the installation by typing:

```
1   vagrant --version
```

The version of Vagrant that you installed should be displayed.

Installation Steps for Linux

For Linux users, the preferred way to install Vagrant is through the package manager of your Linux distribution. Below are the commands for Debian/Ubuntu and Red Hat/CentOS/Fedora distributions.

For Debian/Ubuntu:

```
1   sudo apt update && sudo apt install vagrant
```

For Red Hat/CentOS/Fedora:

```
1   sudo yum install vagrant
```

After installing, you can verify the installation with the following command in your terminal:

```
1   vagrant --version
```

This command will display the currently installed version of Vagrant, confirming that the installation was successful.

Verifying the Installation

Regardless of your operating system, it is important to verify that Vagrant has been correctly installed and is functioning as expected.

The verification step is as simple as running the following command in your terminal or command prompt:

```
1  vagrant --version
```

The output should display the version of Vagrant you have installed, which confirms that the software is ready for use. Here is an example of the expected output:

```
Vagrant 2.2.14
```

With Vagrant successfully installed, you can now proceed to configure and provision virtual development environments as needed. The next sections of this chapter will guide you through utilizing Vagrant to maximize the productivity and flexibility of your development workflows.

1.8 Vagrant Boxes: Overview and Usage

Vagrant boxes form the base image for Vagrant environments, encapsulating operating systems and preconfigured settings into package formats for Vagrant to utilize. These boxes serve as the foundational building blocks for creating reproducible and portable virtual environments, significantly reducing the setup time for development workflows.

A Vagrant box is essentially a snapshot of a virtual machine (VM) at a specific point in time, containing everything needed to run the machine: the operating system, installed software, and configuration settings. This section will delve deeper into the nature of Vagrant boxes, how they are used, and the processes for managing them effectively.

Understanding Vagrant Boxes

The primary purpose of a Vagrant box is to ensure that every member of a development team has a consistent environment. This consistency eliminates the "works on my machine" syndrome, a common problem in software development where code runs on the developer's machine but not on another developer's machine due to environment differences.

To use a Vagrant box, one must initialize a Vagrant environment using a box as the base. This is achieved by specifying the box in a configuration file known as the Vagrantfile. The Vagrantfile contains all the configurations for your Vagrant environment, including the box to use, network settings, shared folders, and provision scripts.

Finding and Adding Boxes

Vagrant boxes can be found in various places, with the most popular source being the public Vagrant Cloud (https://app.vagrantup.com/boxes/search). This repository hosts a wide variety of boxes for different operating systems and configurations. To add a box to your Vagrant environment, you can use the command:

```
1   vagrant box add <box_name>
```

Where <box_name> is the name of the box you wish to add. This command downloads the box to your local machine, making it available for use in your Vagrant environments.

Using a Box

After adding a box to your machine, you can initialize a new Vagrant environment using the box with the following command:

```
1   vagrant init <box_name>
```

This command creates a new Vagrantfile in your current directory, configured to use the specified box. You can then start the Vagrant environment using:

```
1   vagrant up
```

This command reads the Vagrantfile, launches the virtual machine

28

based on the specified box, and configures it according to the settings in the `Vagrantfile`.

Managing Boxes

Vagrant provides several commands to manage boxes, such as updating, removing, and listing available boxes. To update a box to its latest version:

```
1    vagrant box update --box <box_name>
```

To remove a box no longer in use:

```
1    vagrant box remove <box_name>
```

And to list all boxes currently installed on your machine:

```
1    vagrant box list
```

These commands provide the flexibility to manage the boxes your projects depend on efficiently.

Customizing Boxes

Although there are many boxes available, there may be instances where you need a box with a specific configuration that is not readily available. In such cases, you can create a custom Vagrant box. This process involves provisioning a VM to match your requirements, packaging it into a box file, and then adding it to your Vagrant environment. The creation and distribution of custom boxes ensure that development teams can achieve an even higher level of environment standardization.

In summary, Vagrant boxes are pivotal in the creation and management of virtualized development environments with Vagrant. They encapsulate the environment's foundation, ensuring consistency and reducing setup times for development teams. Through a combination of public repositories and the ability to create custom boxes, development teams can tailor their

development environments to match their exact needs, further
enhancing productivity and collaboration.

1.9   Basic Vagrant Commands

Vagrant offers a suite of command-line utilities that facilitate the
lifecycle management of virtual machines. These commands, when
used appropriately, empower developers to swiftly perform
various operations including creating, configuring, connecting to,
and destroying virtual environments. This section will delve into
the fundamental Vagrant commands required to manage these
environments effectively.

- vagrant init: This command initializes a new Vagrant environment by creating a new Vagrantfile in the current directory. The Vagrantfile is a Ruby file used to configure Vagrant
  concerning the requirements of your project. Optionally, this
  command can take a box name and URL as parameters to pre-
  configure the Vagrantfile with a specific box.

```
1   vagrant init hashicorp/bionic64
```

- vagrant up: This command is used to create and configure the
  virtual machine according to the Vagrantfile in the current directory. If the required Vagrant box is not present on the system, Vagrant will automatically download it.

```
1   vagrant up
```

Upon execution, Vagrant initializes the VM and executes any
provisioning scripts defined in the Vagrantfile.

- vagrant ssh: Once the virtual machine is up and running, you
  can connect to it using the vagrant ssh command. This will
  establish a secure shell (SSH) connection to the VM, allowing
  you to execute commands directly on the virtual machine.

```
1   vagrant ssh
```

- vagrant halt: This command is used to gracefully shutdown the running virtual machine. It sends a signal to the operating system to initiate a safe shutdown process.

```
1  vagrant halt
```

- vagrant reload: If you make changes to the Vagrantfile that affect the virtual machine's configuration, vagrant reload will restart the VM, applying any changes made.

```
1  vagrant reload
```

- vagrant destroy: This command stops the running machine and deletes all resources created during the machine creation process. It effectively removes the virtual machine from your system, freeing up resources.

```
1  vagrant destroy
```

A prompt will ask for confirmation before proceeding with the destruction of the VM. To bypass this prompt and destroy the VM immediately, use the -f or --force flag.

- vagrant status: To check the current status of the VMs in your project, use the vagrant status command. It displays information about whether a VM is running, halted, or not created.

```
1  vagrant status
```

- vagrant provision: If provisioning scripts (such as shell scripts, Chef recipes, or Puppet manifests) are defined in your Vagrantfile, the vagrant provision command will execute those scripts on the running VM without restarting or destroying it.

```
1  vagrant provision
```

- vagrant box list: Displays a list of all Vagrant boxes installed on your system.

```
1  vagrant box list
```

31

- `vagrant box update`: Updates the base box used for a Vagrant environment. If a newer version of the box is available, it will be downloaded and used for future creations of the environment.

```
1  vagrant box update
```

- `vagrant plugin`: Manages Vagrant plugins. This encompasses installing, uninstalling, and listing plugins.

```
1  vagrant plugin list
```

It is important for users to familiarize themselves with these commands as they provide the foundational knowledge required to manage and interact with Vagrant environments efficiently. Proficiency in these commands simplifies the process of virtual environment management, thereby streamlining development workflows and enhancing productivity.

1.10   Vagrantfile Explained

In Vagrant, the `Vagrantfile` serves as a pivotal element, acting as the blueprint for configuring virtual environments. This file, written in Ruby, specifies parameters such as the base box to use, the network settings, and the provisioning scripts to be applied to the VM. Understanding the `Vagrantfile` is essential for harnessing the full capability of Vagrant.

Basic Structure

A `Vagrantfile` typically starts with a call to `Vagrant.configure`, specifying the configuration version, most commonly version 2. This is followed by a block that contains the configuration settings for your virtual machine. The structure is as follows:

```
1  Vagrant.configure("2") do |config|
2    # Vagrant and VM configuration settings go here
3  end
```

Specifying a Box

One of the first steps in creating a Vagrant environment is to specify the base box on which your virtual machine will be built. This is done with the following line inside the configuration block:

```
1  config.vm.box = "hashicorp/bionic64"
```

Here, '"hashicorp/bionic64"' represents a specific image of a Linux distribution. You can replace it with the name of any other box available in Vagrant's public box catalog.

Network Configuration

Networking is a critical aspect of any development environment. Vagrant provides straightforward options for network configuration. For example, to enable port forwarding, you can use:

```
1  config.vm.network "forwarded_port", guest: 80, host: 8080
```

This line forwards traffic from port 8080 on the host machine to port 80 on the guest machine, allowing you to access web servers running in your VM via the host's port 8080.

Provisioning Scripts

Vagrant allows you to automatically install software, alter configurations, and more on the machine as part of the vagrant up process through provisioning scripts. Below is an example using a shell script:

```
1  config.vm.provision "shell", inline: <<-SHELL
2    apt-get update
3    apt-get install -y apache2
4  SHELL
```

This will run commands inside the VM to update the package lists and install Apache2.

Synchronization of Folders

By default, Vagrant synchronizes your project directory (where the
Vagrantfile resides) to the '/vagrant' directory in your virtual machine. This behavior ensures that you can easily share files between
the host and the guest machine. The configuration looks like this:

```
1   config.vm.synced_folder ".", "/vagrant"
```

This line means that the current directory ('"."') on the host is synced
with the '/vagrant' directory on the guest.

Running Multiple VMs

Vagrant supports configuring multiple VMs within a single
Vagrantfile. This is achieved by defining multiple configuration
blocks. For example:

```
1   config.vm.define "web" do |web|
2     web.vm.box = "hashicorp/bionic64"
3     web.vm.network "forwarded_port", guest: 80, host: 8080
4   end
5
6   config.vm.define "db" do |db|
7     db.vm.box = "hashicorp/bionic64"
8     db.vm.network "private_network", type: "dhcp"
9   end
```

This sets up two VMs, one intended as a web server and the other as
a database server, each with different networking configurations.

In understanding and manipulating the Vagrantfile, developers
gain control over the virtual environment, tailoring it to the specific
needs of their project. Mastery of the Vagrantfile paves the way
for efficient, consistent, and portable development environments.

1.11 First Steps: Initializing Your First Vagrant Project

Initializing a Vagrant project marks the beginning of simplifying the development environment setup process. This essential step involves creating a basic configuration file, known as `Vagrantfile`, which functions as the blueprint for your Vagrant environment. This file dictates the virtual machine (VM) configurations and provisioning scripts required to prepare the environment. The initialization process can be conducted through a sequence of commands in the terminal or command prompt.

To initiate a new Vagrant project, follow these detailed instructions:

1. Ensure Vagrant is installed on your system. The installation process varies based on the operating system. Refer to the "Installing Vagrant" section for guidance on the installation process.

2. Open a terminal (Linux and macOS) or command prompt (Windows).

3. Navigate to the directory where you wish to create your Vagrant project. This directory will contain the `Vagrantfile` and any other related files for your project.

4. Execute the command `vagrant init`. This command will generate a new `Vagrantfile` in the current directory with default settings. The command can be further specified by providing a box name and version, using the syntax `vagrant init <box_name> <box_version>`. Without specific parameters, Vagrant will generate a `Vagrantfile` with a base box set as `base`, which indicates a placeholder for any specific box.

Upon execution of the `vagrant init` command, the output should resemble the following:

```
A `Vagrantfile` has been placed in this directory. You are now
ready to `vagrant up` your first virtual environment! Please read
the comments in the Vagrantfile as well as documentation on
`vagrantup.com` for more information on using Vagrant.
```

Let's break down the `Vagrantfile` generated. This file is written in Ruby, which allows for dynamic configuration. It begins with a version check to ensure compatibility and might contain configuration blocks for different providers like VirtualBox, Docker, or VMware. The simplicity of the Vagrant architecture is highlighted in the file's comments, guiding users through possible customizations.

```
1   Vagrant.configure("2") do |config|
2     config.vm.box = "base"
3     # Other configuration goes here
4   end
```

The `$config.vm.box` attribute is crucial as it specifies which box (template) to use for the VM. The placeholder `"base"` should be replaced with the name of an actual box that you wish to use. Boxes are essentially snapshots of pre-configured development environments that you can find on Vagrant Cloud or create yourself.

With the `Vagrantfile` in place, the next step is to launch the VM by executing the command `vagrant up`. This process can take several minutes as it involves downloading the specified box (if not already available locally), creating a VM, and configuring it according to the `Vagrantfile`.

To summarize, initializing a Vagrant project simplifies the process of configuring a development environment. It involves creating a `Vagrantfile` which outlines the desired VM configuration and using Vagrant commands to manage the lifecycle of the virtual environment. The ease of use and flexibility provided by Vagrant significantly benefit development workflows by ensuring consistency across multiple environments.

1.12 Benefits of Using Vagrant in Development

The adoption of Vagrant in the development workflow introduces a multitude of benefits designed to streamline the process of software creation, enhance efficiency, and ensure consistency across multiple environments. The following points elucidate the advantages of integrating Vagrant into development routines.

- **Consistency Across Environments:** One of the primary challenges in software development is the "works on my machine" phenomenon, where code behaves differently on various machines due to discrepancies in the operating environment. Vagrant addresses this issue by enabling developers to create and configure lightweight, reproducible, and portable development environments. These environments are defined by code in the Vagrantfile, ensuring that every member of the team is working within an identical setup, thereby significantly reducing environmental discrepancies and integration issues.

- **Ease of Use:** Vagrant is engineered with simplicity in mind. It abstracts away the complexities associated with virtual machines, providing a straightforward command-line interface. For instance, initializing a new Vagrant environment can be done with the mere execution of vagrant up. This simplicity accelerates the setup of development environments, making it accessible even to individuals and teams with minimal experience in managing virtual machines.

```
1  # Initializing a new Vagrant environment
2  vagrant up
```

- **Version Control for Development Environments:** Just as source code is managed through version control, Vagrant allows the environment configuration to be version-controlled. This approach facilitates tracking changes to the environment, reverting to previous versions if necessary, and understanding the evolution of the development setup over time. This capability enhances collaboration among team members and contributes to a more stable and controlled development process.

- **Increased Productivity:** By standardizing the development environment and automating the provisioning process, Vagrant reduces the time developers spend troubleshooting environment-specific issues, allowing them to focus more on writing code. Furthermore, with the provisioning scripts, team members can ramp up on new projects more quickly, since setting up a new development environment can be achieved in a matter of minutes.

- **Compatibility with Multiple Providers:** Vagrant is notably versatile, offering support for various virtualization providers such as VirtualBox, VMware, Hyper-V, and Docker. This flexibility allows teams to select the most suitable provider based on their specific project needs or personal preferences, without being locked into a single solution.

```
# Example showing Vagrant use with different providers
vagrant up --provider=virtualbox
vagrant up --provider=vmware_desktop
vagrant up --provider=hyper_v
```

- **Streamlined Workflow Integration:** Vagrant seamlessly integrates into existing development workflows. Cooperating effortlessly with software configuration management tools like Ansible, Puppet, and Chef, Vagrant facilitates the automation of the provisioning process. This integration ensures that the software environment is not only reproducible but also that it adheres to the practices and standards defined by these tools, further enhancing the development environment's reliability and integrity.

Incorporating Vagrant into development processes yields considerable improvements in environment consistency, ease of use, and overall productivity. By fostering a more efficient, stable, and collaborative development workflow, Vagrant stands as an invaluable tool for both individual developers and teams aiming to optimize their software development practices.

Chapter 2

Setting Up and Configuring Vagrant

Setting up and configuring Vagrant is a critical first step towards leveraging its full potential to create reproducible and portable development environments. This process involves installing Vagrant, selecting a virtualization provider, and configuring the Vagrantfile, which serves as the primary configuration file for defining and managing your virtual machine (VM) environments. Proper setup and configuration ensure that developers can start their projects in environments that closely mimic production systems, thus eliminating the "works on my machine" problem and fostering consistency across development teams. This chapter guides through the essential steps and considerations for setting up Vagrant and configuring it for various development needs.

2.1 Choosing the Right Base Box

Selecting an appropriate base box is a foundational step in setting up a Vagrant environment. A base box essentially serves as the template for the virtual machine (VM) that Vagrant will create and manage. It contains the operating system and potentially a minimal set of software required for the VM to function. The choice of base box can significantly influence the performance, compatibility, and overall development experience. This section will elucidate the various aspects to consider when choosing a base box, ensuring an informed decision is made.

There are several factors to consider when selecting a base box:

- **Operating System**: The base box should match the operating system that closely replicates the production environment or the one most familiar to the development team.

- **Size**: Heavier boxes come with more pre-installed packages and features but consume more resources. Opting for a lightweight box might require additional setup time but can lead to a more efficient development process.

- **Provider Compatibility**: Ensure the base box is compatible with the virtualization provider (VirtualBox, VMware, Hyper-V, etc.) being used.

- **Community Support and Updates**: Choose a base box that is actively maintained and supported by a robust community. Regular updates suggest strong community involvement and a lower risk of security vulnerabilities.

- **Licensing**: Ensure the base box and its contents comply with licensing requirements, particularly for commercial projects.

To find a base box, the Vagrant Cloud (`https://app.vagrantup.com/boxes/search`) serves as the primary repository. It allows users to search through a vast collection of base boxes using various filters such as provider, version, and operating system. For example, to search for an Ubuntu 20.04 box compatible with VirtualBox, the following command can be executed in the terminal:

```
1   vagrant box add ubuntu/focal64 --provider=virtualbox
```

After executing this command, Vagrant will download the specified box and add it to your list of available boxes. You can verify the successful addition by listing all available boxes:

```
1  vagrant box list
```

If the addition was successful, you should see 'ubuntu/focal64' listed among the available boxes. It is worth noting that the name 'ubuntu/focal64' refers to the official Ubuntu 20.04 LTS (Focal Fossa) box for VirtualBox. This naming convention helps in identifying the operating system, version, and intended provider.

When configuring the `Vagrantfile`, assign the chosen box to the `config.vm.box` setting:

```
1  Vagrant.configure("2") do |config|
2    config.vm.box = "ubuntu/focal64"
3  end
```

This line instructs Vagrant to use 'ubuntu/focal64' as the base box for the VM being configured.

In summary, the selection of the right base box is pivotal for setting up a Vagrant environment that is efficient, secure, and compatible with the development team's needs. By considering the factors outlined above and utilizing the Vagrant Cloud for discovery, developers can make informed decisions that facilitate seamless and productive workflows.

2.2 Configuring the Vagrantfile: Basics

Configuring the Vagrantfile is a fundamental process that dictates how a virtual machine (VM) is set up, provisioned, and managed through Vagrant. This file, written in Ruby syntax, allows developers to specify the VM's properties such as the base box, networking configurations, synced folders, and provisioning scripts among others. Understanding the structure and basic settings of the Vagrantfile is key to effectively leveraging Vagrant's capabilities.

Firstly, to initialize a new Vagrantfile in your project directory, the following command must be executed in the terminal:

```
1   $ vagrant init <base_box_name>
```

This command creates a Vagrantfile in the directory if one does not already exist, and sets the base box for the VM using the specified <base_box_name>.

The initial structure of a Vagrantfile looks as follows:

```
1   Vagrant.configure("2") do |config|
2     config.vm.box = "<base_box_name>"
3   end
```

In this configuration, Vagrant.configure("2") specifies the configuration version (currently version 2 is used for compatibility with Vagrant 1.1 and later). The block given to the configuration method, do |config|, is where all configuration for the Vagrant environment is done.

Particularly, config.vm.box assigns the base box that the VM will use as its underlying system. This is a critical setting and often the first line modified in a new Vagrantfile.

Further customization can be done to specify the VM's provider-specific settings. For example, to customize VirtualBox settings:

```
1   config.vm.provider "virtualbox" do |vb|
2     vb.name = "MyVM"
3     vb.memory = 2048
4     vb.cpus = 2
5   end
```

This block configures the VirtualBox VM with the name "MyVM", sets its memory to 2048 MB, and allocates 2 CPUs to it.

Networking is another crucial aspect configured in the Vagrantfile. To enable port forwarding from the host to the VM:

```
1   config.vm.network "forwarded_port", guest: 80, host: 8080
```

This line forwards traffic from port 8080 on the host to port 80 on the VM, allowing you to access services running on the VM through localhost:8080 on your host machine.

Synced folders enable seamless file sharing between the host and the VM, simplifying development workflows. By default, Vagrant syncs the project directory to /vagrant within the VM:

```
1  config.vm.synced_folder ".", "/vagrant"
```

Lastly, provisioning scripts automate the installation and configuration of software within the VM. For instance, using a shell script:

```
1  config.vm.provision "shell", inline: <<-SHELL
2    apt-get update
3    apt-get install -y apache2
4  SHELL
```

This provisioner runs the specified shell commands within the VM, installing Apache2 in this example.

To summarize, the Vagrantfile is a comprehensive tool for configuring VMs, allowing developers to dictate everything from hardware specifications to software provisioning. Understanding its syntax and options is crucial for effectively utilizing Vagrant to manage development environments.

2.3   Networking Options in Vagrant

Networking in Vagrant provides several methods for configuring network interfaces in your virtual machine environments to enhance communication with the host machine, other virtual machines, and the outside world. Properly understanding and configuring networking is essential for tasks such as API testing, running servers, or even for systems that require communication between multiple virtual machines. This section will discuss the main networking options available in Vagrant: forwarded ports, private networks, and public networks.

Forwarded Ports Configuration

Forwarded ports allow access to a specific port within the virtual machine from the host machine. This is particularly useful for accessing web servers running inside the virtual machine from your host machine's browser.

To configure forwarded ports, you must update the `Vagrantfile` with specific parameters. Here's an example illustrating how to forward port 80 from the guest to port 8080 on the host:

```
1  Vagrant.configure("2") do |config|
2    config.vm.network "forwarded_port", guest: 80, host: 8080
3  end
```

This configuration will redirect all traffic from the host machine on port 8080 to port 80 on the virtual machine.

Private Network Configuration

A private network allows for the creation of a network only accessible to the host machine and any other machines within the same private network. This can be useful for simulating multi-server environments.

Setting up a private network in Vagrant is straightforward. Add the following lines to your `Vagrantfile`:

```
1  Vagrant.configure("2") do |config|
2    config.vm.network "private_network", type: "dhcp"
3  end
```

This configuration leverages DHCP to automatically assign an IP address to the virtual machine. For a static IP, replace the `"dhcp"` directive with `ip: "192.168.33.10"`, for example.

Public Network Configuration

Public networks expose your virtual machine to the local network, making it accessible from other machines on the same network. This is ideal for showcasing applications running within the VM to colleagues or for testing applications across different devices.

To configure a public network, insert the following snippet into your `Vagrantfile`:

```
1  Vagrant.configure("2") do |config|
2    config.vm.network "public_network"
3  end
```

Be aware that enabling a public network might require additional network configurations or even administrative permissions depending on your network setup.

Vagrant's networking capabilities offer flexibility in configuring the virtual machine's network according to the project's needs. Choosing the correct networking configuration will depend on whether you need to expose your application to the outside world, require connectivity between the host and the VM, or between multiple VMs in a private network. Proper attention to detail in this aspect will ensure seamless development and testing environments that mimic production settings.

2.4   Forwarded Ports Configuration

Forwarded ports in Vagrant play a pivotal role in establishing a communication bridge between the host machine and the virtual machine (VM). This mechanism allows services running within the VM to be accessible from the host machine using specified port numbers. Configuring port forwarding is essential for tasks such as viewing a web application in a browser on your host machine that is actually running inside the VM.

The configuration of forwarded ports is primarily handled within the 'Vagrantfile', a Ruby file used for specifying the configuration details of the VMs managed by Vagrant. The syntax for forwarding a port is straightforward and can be encapsulated in the following structure:

```
1  config.vm.network "forwarded_port", guest: <guest_port>, host: <host_port>
```

In this structure, `<guest_port>` refers to the port number on the VM that will be forwarded, and `<host_port>` specifies the port on the host machine to which the guest's port will map. It's critical to ensure that the chosen host port does not conflict with any services already running on the host machine to prevent any connectivity issues.

A practical example of port forwarding configuration is for a web application running on port 8080 within the VM. To make this application accessible from the host machine's browser, the following configuration block would be added to the 'Vagrantfile':

```
1   config.vm.network "forwarded_port", guest: 8080, host: 8081
```

This configuration means the application running inside the VM on port 8080 can be accessed from the host machine using the URL `http://localhost:8081`. It is essential to understand that the port numbers (both guest and host) in the example are arbitrary and can be adjusted based on the application requirements and available ports on the host machine.

To ensure the changes take effect, after adjusting the 'Vagrantfile', the VM needs to be reloaded. This can be achieved by running the following command from the terminal:

```
1   vagrant reload
```

This command makes Vagrant halt the running VM, apply the configuration changes, and then start the VM again. Alternatively, for newly added forwarded ports, using the command `vagrant reload --provision` ensures that any provisioners run again, allowing for a complete reconfiguration based on the updated settings.

Configuring forwarded ports in Vagrant is straightforward yet crucial for facilitating the access of services running inside the VM from the host machine. The flexibility in choosing port numbers allows for easy integration into existing development workflows and enhances the utility of Vagrant-managed virtual environments.

2.5   Private Network Configuration

In this section, we will discuss the process of setting up a private network for a virtual machine managed by Vagrant. This configuration enables the host machine to communicate with the guest VM on a network that is not accessible from outside the host machine, providing an isolated environment for development.

First, we must understand the purpose of a private network setup. It creates a network interface on the guest VM that only the host machine can access. This setup is particularly useful for running server applications on the guest that only need to be accessed by the host.

To configure a private network, we need to edit the `Vagrantfile` within our Vagrant project directory. The `Vagrantfile` is a Ruby file used to configure Vagrant on a per-project basis.

The basic command to configure a private network is as follows:

```
1   config.vm.network "private_network", ip: "192.168.50.4"
```

In the example above, `"private_network"` specifies that we are creating a private network. The `ip` option assigns a static IP address to the guest VM. It is essential to choose an IP address that does not conflict with the host's existing network interfaces or any other VMs that might be running.

For cases where static IP assignment is not necessary, and DHCP can be used for automatic IP allocation, the configuration simplifies to:

```
1   config.vm.network "private_network", type: "dhcp"
```

This configuration instructs Vagrant to request an IP from the DHCP server configured for the private network. This approach is beneficial when managing multiple VMs or when the specific IP address of a VM is not critical.

After modifying the `Vagrantfile`, the changes need to be applied by restarting the Vagrant environment. This typically involves running the following commands:

```
vagrant reload
```

49

The `vagrant reload` command will restart your Vagrant machine, applying any changes to the `Vagrantfile`, including network configurations.

In some scenarios, it may be necessary to enable additional network services, such as a DNS server on the private network. While Vagrant does not natively manage these services, they can be configured within the guest VM or by using provisioning scripts.

Upon successful setup, the host machine can communicate with the guest VM using the configured IP address. It facilitates scenarios where applications running within the VM need to be accessed locally for development, testing, or debugging purposes.

In summary, configuring a private network in Vagrant involves the following steps:

- Editing the `Vagrantfile` to include a private network configuration.

- Assigning an IP address, either static or via DHCP.

- Reloading the Vagrant environment to apply changes.

It is important to note that while private networks facilitate isolated communication between host and guest, they do not provide Internet access for the VM. If external network access is required from within the VM, alternative or additional network configurations, such as public networking, should be considered.

2.6   Public Network Configuration

In this section we will discuss the configuration of public networks within the Vagrant environment. Connecting your virtual machines (VMs) to a public network means they can be accessed from other machines on the same network, and, if correctly configured, from the internet. This feature is particularly useful for simulating production environments where services are exposed to external traffic.

The basic directive for configuring a public network in your Vagrantfile is the config.vm.network method, which takes 'public_network' as its first argument. Additional options can be specified to customize the network setup as needed.

Let's start with a simple example of enabling a public network without any specific options:

```
1  Vagrant.configure("2") do |config|
2    config.vm.box = "base"
3    config.vm.network "public_network"
4  end
```

This configuration will prompt Vagrant to use the default bridge network available on the host machine. However, in most cases, you might need or want to specify certain options like the IP address or which bridge interface to use. Here's how you can assign a specific IP address to your VM:

```
1  Vagrant.configure("2") do |config|
2    config.vm.box = "base"
3    config.vm.network "public_network", ip: "192.168.0.17"
4  end
```

In some scenarios, it might be necessary to explicitly specify the bridge adapter. The name of the adapter can vary depending on your host operating system and network setup. Here's an example:

```
1  Vagrant.configure("2") do |config|
2    config.vm.box = "base"
3    config.vm.network "public_network", bridge: "en0: Wi-Fi (AirPort)"
4  end
```

Depending on the OS and Vagrant versions, you might encounter issues with automatic bridge selection. This method allows you to specify the interface manually, circumventing such problems.

Another important aspect of public networking in Vagrant is the ability to use DHCP to dynamically assign an IP address to your VM. This is done by omitting the IP address option:

```
1  Vagrant.configure("2") do |config|
2    config.vm.box = "base"
3    config.vm.network "public_network", use_dhcp_assigned_default_route: true
4  end
```

However, using DHCP might complicate accessing your VM from the host machine since the IP can change upon each boot. It's often a trade-off between convenience and predictability.

After configuring the public network, to apply the changes, you must either start the VM if it's not running with `vagrant up` or reload the VM configuration with `vagrant reload` if it's already running. Upon execution, Vagrant might prompt you to choose which network interface you wish to bridge with. It's important to select the correct interface that corresponds to your desired network connection.

Here is an output example when you are prompted during a `vagrant up` or `vagrant reload` process:

```
==> default: Available bridged network interfaces:
1) en0: Wi-Fi (AirPort)
2) en1: Thunderbolt 1
3) en2: Thunderbolt 2
4) bridge0
5) p2p0
6) awdl0
7) llw0
8) en5: USB 10/100/1000 LAN
9) en4: Thunderbolt 3 .
==> default: When choosing an interface, it is usually the one that is
==> default: being used to connect to the internet.
```

Configuring public networks in Vagrant enables external access to the VMs, simulating a more realistic environment closer to production. Remember to carefully choose the network settings based on your project requirements and network infrastructure to ensure seamless connectivity and access.

2.7   Synced Folders: Setup and Options

Synced folders in Vagrant are an essential mechanism allowing files to be shared between the host machine and the guest virtual machine. This feature facilitates seamless file exchange and editing, enabling developers to use tools on their host machine while keeping the files in sync with the guest machine. This section will discuss how to set up and configure synced folders in Vagrant, alongside exploring the various options available.

To activate a synced folder, it is necessary to modify the `Vagrantfile` configuration. The `Vagrantfile` is a Ruby script used to configure Vagrant environments. By specifying the synced folder settings within this file, users can define the paths on the host and the guest that should be synchronized.

The basic configuration syntax for enabling a synced folder in your `Vagrantfile` is as follows:

```
1  Vagrant.configure("2") do |config|
2    config.vm.synced_folder "host/folder/path", "/guest/folder/path"
3  end
```

In this code snippet, '"host/folder/path"' should be replaced with the path to the folder on the host machine that you wish to share with the guest machine. Similarly, '"/guest/folder/path"' should be replaced with the intended path on the guest machine where the host's files will be accessible.

Vagrant offers several options to customize the behavior and performance of synced folders. These options can be passed as a third argument in the form of a hash to the `config.vm.synced_folder` method. Here are some common options:

- `disabled: true` - If set to true, this option disables the synced folder.

- `type: "nfs"` - This specifies the type of synced folder. By default, Vagrant uses its native synced folders, but users can specify others like NFS, SMB, or rsync.

- `owner: "vagrant"` - This sets the owner of the files in the guest machine. By default, it is set to the SSH user.

- `group: "vagrant"` - Similar to `owner`, this option sets the group ownership of the synced folder in the guest machine.

- `mount_options: ["dmode=777", "fmode=666"]` - This allows for custom mount options to be passed to the underlying technology powering the synced folder.

It's also possible to configure multiple synced folders by repeating the `config.vm.synced_folder` method with different paths and options. For instance:

```
1  Vagrant.configure("2") do |config|
2    config.vm.synced_folder "src/", "/home/vagrant/code",
3      owner: "vagrant", group: "vagrant"
4
5    config.vm.synced_folder "data/", "/home/vagrant/data",
6      type: "nfs"
7  end
```

This configuration sets up two synced folders, each with tailored options to suit different requirements; one uses Vagrant's default syncing mechanism, while the other operates over NFS for improved performance.

It is crucial to consider the performance implications of the various synced folder types. The default sync method is convenient and works out of the box on all supported Vagrant platforms but may not offer the best performance for large datasets or high-frequency file operations. Alternatives like NFS or rsync could provide substantial performance benefits but may require additional configuration on the host and guest machines.

In summary, configuring synced folders in Vagrant is straightforward and highly customizable. By tailoring the synced folder options to the specific needs of your development environment, you can ensure efficient and seamless file synchronization between the host and guest machines.

2.8   Provisioning with Shell Scripts

Provisioning in the context of Vagrant involves the automatic setup and configuration of a virtual machine (VM) according to predefined specifications. One of the most straightforward and commonly used methods for provisioning is the use of shell scripts. Shell scripts allow the execution of a series of commands on the VM, facilitating the installation of software, configuration of settings, and much more.

To provision a VM using shell scripts, one must first ensure that the necessary script(s) are created. These scripts should include all command-line instructions required for setting up the VM environment. Once the script is ready, it can be integrated into the Vagrant environment through modifications to the `Vagrantfile`.

Configuring the `Vagrantfile` for Shell Provisioning

To instruct Vagrant to use a shell script for provisioning, the following configuration must be added to the `Vagrantfile`:

```
1  Vagrant.configure("2") do |config|
2    # Specify the base box
3    config.vm.box = "base_box_name"
4
5    # Provisioning configuration
6    config.vm.provision "shell", path: "path/to/script.sh"
7  end
```

In the above code snippet, `"shell"` specifies that shell provisioning should be used, and `path: "path/to/script.sh"` denotes the relative or absolute path to the shell script that should be executed.

Inline Shell Provisioning

Aside from specifying an external script file, Vagrant also allows for inline shell provisioning, where the script is directly included in the `Vagrantfile`. This can be particularly useful for shorter scripts or when wishing to keep the provisioning instructions close to the VM configuration.

```
1  Vagrant.configure("2") do |config|
2    config.vm.box = "base_box_name"
3
4    config.vm.provision "shell", inline: <<-SHELL
5      apt-get update
6      apt-get install -y apache2
7    SHELL
8  end
```

The above example demonstrates an inline shell provisioning block that updates the package lists for upgrades and installs Apache2 on a Debian or Ubuntu-based system.

Important Considerations

When using shell scripts for provisioning, it is crucial to consider the following:

- Idempotency: Scripts should be idempotent, meaning running the script multiple times on the same VM does not alter the system state beyond the first application. This principle ensures that repeated provisions do not lead to unintended changes or configurations.

- Shell Compatibility: Ensure that the shell script is compatible with the default shell on the VM. Most Linux distributions use bash, but variations may exist. Specifying the interpreter in the script's shebang line can mitigate potential issues.

- Error Handling: Incorporate error checking and handling into the script to avoid provisioning failures. Use exit statuses and conditional statements to manage errors and ensure that the provisioning process can gracefully recover or halt upon encountering critical issues.

Example Shell Script

Below is an example shell script named `provision.sh`, designed to install and start a simple web server:

```
 1  #!/bin/bash
 2  set -e
 3
 4  # Update system package repository
 5  apt-get update
 6
 7  # Install nginx
 8  apt-get install -y nginx
 9
10  # Start nginx service
11  systemctl start nginx
```

To apply this provisioning script within a Vagrantfile, the path configuration would be:

```
 1  config.vm.provision "shell", path: "provision.sh"
```

The script ensures that the system's package repository is updated, installs Nginx, and starts the Nginx service. Incorporating error handling with `set -e` causes the script to exit immediately if any command exits with a non-zero status.

Effective provisioning with shell scripts can significantly streamline the setup of VMs, making the development environment more predictable and consistent across different machines. By following the guidelines and practices outlined in this section, developers can harness the power of shell scripting to automate the provisioning process in Vagrant.

2.9   Using Ansible for Provisioning

Provisioning virtual machines (VMs) efficiently is a cornerstone of ensuring that development environments are set up with consistency, speed, and accuracy.   Ansible, an open-source automation tool, provides a powerful method for achieving this through its simple, yet potent, automation and orchestration capabilities.   This section explains the procedures and considerations involved in using Ansible for the provisioning of VMs in Vagrant.

Firstly, it is crucial to understand the mechanism by which Vagrant and Ansible interact. Vagrant acts as the orchestrator that prepares VMs, whereas Ansible serves as the provisioner that configures these VMs to a desired state by running Ansible playbooks. An Ansible playbook is essentially a YAML file that defines the work tasks to be executed on the VMs.

Before integrating Ansible with Vagrant, ensure that Ansible is installed on the host system. Installation details are outside the scope of this text but can be found on the official Ansible documentation website.

Once Ansible is installed, the next step involves setting up the Vagrant environment to use Ansible for provisioning. This is achieved by specifying the `ansible` provisioning method in the `Vagrantfile`.

Here is an example configuration:

```
1  Vagrant.configure("2") do |config|
2    config.vm.box = "ubuntu/bionic64"
3
4    config.vm.provision "ansible" do |ansible|
5      ansible.playbook = "playbook.yml"
6    end
7  end
```

In this example, the `ansible.playbook` attribute points to the location of the Ansible playbook file that will be executed when the VM is provisioned. It's important to ensure that the playbook file (`playbook.yml` in this example) exists and is accessible from the location where the Vagrant command is run.

Next, let's delve into the structure of an Ansible playbook that could be used in provisioning. Consider the following simple playbook that installs Apache on an Ubuntu VM:

```
1  ---
2  - hosts: all
3    become: yes
4    tasks:
5    - name: Install Apache
6      apt:
7        name: apache2
8        state: present
```

This playbook contains a single task named "Install Apache", which uses the `apt` module to ensure that the Apache package (`apache2`) is installed. The playbook is designed to be idempotent, meaning running it multiple times on the same system will produce the same outcome, making it ideal for provisioning scenarios.

For scenarios requiring advanced provisioning, Ansible offers a vast array of modules and roles to automate various tasks such as package installation, user creation, and file management. It also supports complex orchestration using conditionals, loops, and variables to tailor the environment as needed.

In addition to the basic setup, Vagrant supports further customization of the Ansible provisioning process through additional configuration options. For instance, you can specify extra options to be passed to Ansible with the `ansible.extra_args` configuration, or define a specific inventory file using the `ansible.inventory_path` option.

By leveraging Ansible for provisioning with Vagrant, developers and operations teams can automate the creation and configuration of their development, testing, and production environments in a repeatable and reliable manner. This not only improves efficiency but also ensures consistency across different stages of the software development lifecycle.

The integration of Ansible into the Vagrant workflow enhances the flexibility and power of managing VMs. Through the use of playbooks, the setup and configuration of environments become streamlined, fostering a DevOps culture that emphasizes automation, collaboration, and speed.

2.10   Integrating Puppet and Chef

Integrating Puppet and Chef with Vagrant is a technique utilized to automate the provisioning of virtual machines, ensuring that the software and configuration within these VMs are consistent and reproducible. Both Puppet and Chef are powerful configuration management tools that allow for the automation of the setup and maintenance of software on multiple machines, making them invaluable in a development workflow that aims for high efficiency and reliability.

Puppet Integration

To incorporate Puppet into a Vagrant environment, the configuration specifics are provided within the `Vagrantfile`. This setup enables the Puppet manifest files, which define the system configuration, to be automatically applied when the VM is provisioned.

The basic structure for integrating Puppet is as follows:

```
1  config.vm.provision "puppet" do |puppet|
2    puppet.manifest_file = "default.pp"
3    puppet.manifests_path = "manifests"
```

```
4    puppet.module_path = "modules"
5    puppet.options = "--verbose --debug"
6    end
```

In the above configuration:

- `manifest_file` specifies the entry point for the Puppet scripts. The `default.pp` file is commonly used as the main manifest file.

- `manifests_path` defines the directory where Puppet looks for manifest files.

- `module_path` indicates where Puppet should find modules, which are collections of resources that are used in the provisioning process.

- `options` allows specifying additional options to the Puppet command. The use of `--verbose --debug` is helpful for troubleshooting.

Chef Integration

Similar to Puppet, Chef can also be seamlessly integrated into Vagrant using the `Vagrantfile`. This integration facilitates the use of Chef recipes and cookbooks, which detail the configuration management tasks, to provision the VMs.

The typical configuration for Chef integration is exemplified below:

```
1    config.vm.provision "chef_solo" do |chef|
2      chef.cookbooks_path = ["./cookbooks"]
3      chef.roles_path = "roles"
4      chef.data_bags_path = "data_bags"
5      chef.recipes = ["apache", "mysql", "php"]
6    end
```

In this configuration:

- `cookbooks_path` directs Chef to the location of the cookbooks, which contain recipes that specify how to configure the software and systems.

- `roles_path` points to the directory where roles are defined. Roles allow the grouping of configurations and are useful for managing complex environments.

- `data_bags_path` specifies where data bags are located. Data bags store global variables as JSON data and are accessible from Chef recipes.

- `recipes` is an array that lists the names of the recipes to be applied to the VM. This example applies the `apache`, `mysql`, and `php` recipes.

For both Puppet and Chef, the integration with Vagrant not only automates the provisioning of VMs but also ensures that the configurations are version-controlled, making it easy to reproduce environments across different development setups. This uniformity eliminates inconsistencies and promotes collaboration across development teams by providing a shared understanding of the environment setup.

2.11   Customizing the VM: CPU and Memory

To tailor a virtual machine (VM) to meet specific developmental or testing requirements, adjusting its resources like CPU and memory is imperative. Vagrant enables easy customization of these parameters through its primary configuration file, the Vagrantfile. This section elucidates the process of specifying the CPU and memory allocation for your VMs, leveraging the capabilities of different providers such as VirtualBox, VMWare, and Hyper-V.

Customizing CPU and memory settings optimizes the performance of VMs and ensures they mimic production environments as closely as possible, providing a reliable development setting. This involves editing the Vagrantfile to include specific configuration commands depending on the chosen provider.

VirtualBox

For VirtualBox users, customizing CPU and memory settings
involves adding or altering the vb.customize method within the
Vagrantfile. The following example demonstrates how to assign 2
CPU cores and 4GB of memory to a VM:

```
Vagrant.configure("2") do |config|
  config.vm.box = "base"

  config.vm.provider "virtualbox" do |vb|
    # Customize the number of CPUs
    vb.customize ["modifyvm", :id, "--cpus", "2"]

    # Customize the amount of memory
    vb.customize ["modifyvm", :id, "--memory", "4096"]
  end
end
```

VMWare

For those using VMWare, the process is quite similar, with minor differences in syntax. The VMware plugin provides a convenient way
to specify these resources:

```
Vagrant.configure("2") do |config|
  config.vm.box = "base"

  config.vm.provider "vmware_fusion" do |v|
    v.vmx["numvcpus"] = "2"
    v.vmx["memsize"] = "4096"
  end
end
```

Here, the vmx configuration file is directly edited to set the number
of CPUs and the memory size.

Hyper-V

Configuring CPU and memory for VMs under Hyper-V involves a
slightly different approach. Hyper-V's integration with Vagrant allows for direct specification of these properties:

```
Vagrant.configure("2") do |config|
```

```
2    config.vm.box = "base"
3
4    config.vm.provider "hyperv" do |hv|
5      hv.cpus = 2
6      hv.memory = 4096
7    end
8  end
```

This concise syntax is a straightforward way of assigning resources to your VM under Hyper-V.

Validation of Configuration

After customizing the CPU and memory settings of your VM, it is crucial to validate the configuration to ensure the VM starts with the intended resources. This can be achieved by accessing the VM's settings through the provider's GUI or CLI. For VirtualBox, for example, you can verify the settings through the Oracle VM VirtualBox Manager. Alternatively, for a command-line verification method, the following command can be used in the terminal:

```
1  VBoxManage showvminfo <vm_name> | grep -E "Memory size|Number of CPUs"
```

This command outputs the allocated memory size and number of CPUs for the specified VM, allowing for a simple validation of your configuration.

Adjusting Configuration for Optimal Performance

It is worth noting that while increasing CPU and memory allocations can enhance VM performance, these resources should be allocated judiciously, keeping in mind the host machine's limits. Allocating too much memory or too many CPUs to a VM can lead to suboptimal performance of both the host system and the VM. Therefore, it is recommended to start with conservative settings and gradually adjust based on performance observations and requirements.

Customizing the CPU and memory for your VMs in Vagrant is a crucial step in creating a development environment that closely mirrors production systems. By carefully adjusting these settings as described, developers can ensure their VMs are both high performing and resource-efficient, leading to a more seamless and effective development workflow.

2.12 Multi-Machine Setup: Defining Multiple VMs in a Single Vagrantfile

Multi-machine setup in Vagrant allows the definition and management of multiple virtual machines (VMs) within a single Vagrantfile. This capability is particularly useful for developing and testing applications that are designed to run on different servers or for simulating a multi-server environment on a local development machine.

To configure multiple VMs, the Vagrantfile must include a specific configuration block for each VM. These blocks are defined using the config.vm.define method, which takes the name of the VM as a parameter, followed by a block of settings that apply to that particular VM.

The following example illustrates the basic structure for defining two VMs within a single Vagrantfile:

```
1   Vagrant.configure("2") do |config|
2
3     # Configuration for the first VM
4     config.vm.define "web" do |web|
5       web.vm.box = "ubuntu/bionic64"
6       web.vm.network "forwarded_port", guest: 80, host: 8080
7       web.vm.provision "shell", inline: "apt-get update && apt-get install -y nginx
        "
8     end
9
10    # Configuration for the second VM
11    config.vm.define "db" do |db|
12      db.vm.box = "ubuntu/bionic64"
13      db.vm.network "private_network", ip: "192.168.50.4"
14      db.vm.provision "shell", inline: <<-SHELL
15        apt-get update
16        apt-get install -y mysql-server
17      SHELL
18    end
19
20  end
```

In the above example, two VMs are defined: one named web and the other named db. Both VMs are based on the same box (ubuntu/bionic64), but they are configured differently. The web VM has a forwarded port configuration allowing HTTP traffic on port 80 inside the VM to be accessed via port 8080 on the host machine. It also installs Nginx using a shell provisioner. The db VM, on the other hand, is setup with a private network IP and installs MySQL server.

When defining multiple VMs, each VM can be individually configured with its unique settings, such as network configurations, synced folders, and provisioners. This allows for a high degree of flexibility and control over the development environment setup.

To operate on a specific VM from the command line, the VM's name (as defined in the Vagrantfile) must be specified. For instance, to bring up the web VM, the command would be:

```
vagrant up web
```

Similarly, to SSH into the db VM, the command would be:

```
vagrant ssh db
```

This selective control over VMs simplifies the process of managing a complex environment with different types of servers or configurations. Additionally, using a single Vagrantfile for multiple VMs aids in maintaining consistency across different environments and streamlines the setup process for new developers joining a project.

Lastly, it is worth mentioning that while defining multiple VMs in a single Vagrantfile is convenient for many scenarios, it is important to be mindful of the host machine's resources. Each VM consumes CPU, memory, and disk space, so it is crucial to ensure the host machine has sufficient resources to support the desired number of VMs without degradation in performance.

2.13   Post-Installation Scripts and Tips

Once the Vagrant environment has been established, the addition of post-installation scripts can enhance and automate the setup of the virtual machine (VM). Post-installation scripts execute commands inside the VM after its initial provisioning, enabling tasks such as updating software packages, installing additional tools, or configuring system settings without manual intervention. This section will explore various practices and tips for utilizing post-installation scripts efficiently in Vagrant.

First, let's address how to include a post-installation script in the Vagrant setup. This is achieved by editing the `Vagrantfile` and using the `shell` provisioner. The provisioner allows the execution of shell commands or scripts on the VM. Here is an example incorporating a post-installation script:

```
1  Vagrant.configure("2") do |config|
2    config.vm.box = "ubuntu/bionic64"
3
4    config.vm.provision "shell", inline: <<-SHELL
5      apt-get update
6      apt-get install -y nginx
7      echo "Installed Nginx" > /var/www/html/index.html
8    SHELL
9  end
```

In the code above, the shell provisioner is used to run commands that update the package list of the Ubuntu system, install Nginx, and then place a text file in the web server's root directory. This kind of script is particularly useful for automating the installation of software and initial configuration of the VM.

Moreover, for more complex provisioning tasks, it is possible and often preferable to reference an external script instead of using inline commands:

```
1  config.vm.provision "shell", path: "bootstrap.sh"
```

Where `bootstrap.sh` is a shell script located in the same directory as the `Vagrantfile`. This approach keeps the Vagrantfile cleaner and allows for more complex scripts that are easier to maintain and understand.

Efficient use of post-installation scripts also requires understanding how to optimize their execution. Since these scripts are re-executed every time the VM is provisioned, idempotent scripts (scripts that can be run multiple times without changing the system beyond the initial application) are crucial. This prevents issues such as duplicated installations or configurations. Here's a simple approach to ensuring a command is idempotent:

```
1  if ! command -v nginx >/dev/null; then
2    apt-get update
3    apt-get install -y nginx
4  fi
```

This snippet checks if Nginx is already installed ('command -v nginx >/dev/null' returns true if it is) and only proceeds with the update and installation commands if it is not.

Furthermore, error handling within scripts can prevent provisioning errors from halting the VM setup. A simple strategy is to use the shell set options, such as '-e', which causes the script to exit immediately if a command exits with a non-zero status:

```
1  set -e
2  # Proceed with commands
```

Lastly, a noteworthy tip for leveraging post-installation scripts is to periodically review and update them to reflect the latest packages and avoid deprecated or outdated configurations. This ensures that the environment remains secure and efficient.

Post-installation scripts offer a powerful method for customizing and automating Vagrant environments post-setup. By following best practices for crafting these scripts—such as using external files for complex scripts, ensuring idempotency, implementing error handling, and keeping scripts updated—developers can significantly streamline their development processes.

2.14   Version Control for Vagrantfiles

Version control systems (VCS) are essential tools for software development, offering a means to track and manage changes to code over time. The integration of VCS with Vagrant environments, through the management of Vagrantfile configurations, is a critical practice that enhances collaboration, ensures consistency, and facilitates the easy rollback of changes when necessary.

A Vagrantfile is a Ruby file used to configure Vagrant environments. It includes instructions for Vagrant on how to set up and provision virtual machines according to the project's requirements. Given its importance in defining development, staging, and production environments, version controlling this file alongside your project code is recommended.

- *Enhancing Collaboration*:   When working in a team, the Vagrantfile should be accessible to all team members. By versioning this file, any changes made to the environment setup can be shared across the team, ensuring that everyone is working within the same configuration. This eradicates the "works on my machine" syndrome by maintaining a consistent environment across different workstations.

- *Tracking Changes and Facilitating Rollbacks*:   Version control allows you to keep a history of modifications made to the Vagrantfile. If a change leads to issues or conflicts within the development environment, it is straightforward to revert to a previous version of the file where the environments were stable.

- *Simplifying Environment Setup for New Team Members*:   New members joining a project can set up their development environment by cloning the project repository and running vagrant up. This process dramatically reduces the time taken to onboard new developers, as they do not need to manually configure their machines to match the project's requirements.

Best Practices for Version Controlling `Vagrantfile`

1. **Commit Often**: Regularly commit changes to the `Vagrantfile` when modifications are made to the environment. This practice ensures a proper history is maintained, facilitating easier troubleshooting and understanding of the environment's evolution over time.

2. **Use Branching**: When experimenting with new features or setups, use branches to keep the mainline stable. Merge the changes back into the main branch once they are tested and confirmed to work as expected. This approach keeps the primary development environment stable while allowing for experimentation.

3. **Include Clear Commit Messages**: Every commit should include a clear message that describes the changes made to the `Vagrantfile`. This clarity aids in understanding the purpose of each change, particularly when reviewing the history of the file.

4. **Ignore Sensitive Data**: Ensure that sensitive data, such as API keys or passwords, is not stored within the `Vagrantfile` itself. Instead, use environment variables or separate configuration files that are not version-controlled to manage sensitive information securely.

Version controlling the `Vagrantfile` is a practice that aligns with the broader principles of infrastructure as code (IaC), treating the configuration of virtual environments with the same care as application code. By following the highlighted guidelines, teams can enhance the reliability and consistency of their development environments, contributing significantly to the success of their projects.

Chapter 3

Provisioning in Vagrant

Provisioning in Vagrant is a mechanism that automates the installation and configuration of software on the virtual machine once it's created, allowing developers to quickly set up their development environments according to the project's requirements. This automation is achieved through the use of provisioning scripts or configuration management tools such as Ansible, Chef, Puppet, or simple shell scripts. By automating this process, Vagrant ensures that the development environment is not only consistent across different machines but can also be recreated at any time with minimal effort. This chapter delves into the various provisioning methods supported by Vagrant, demonstrating how to efficiently automate the environment setup.

3.1   Understanding Provisioning in Vagrant

Provisioning within the context of Vagrant is a critical concept that facilitates the automated setup of development environments. At its core, provisioning refers to the process of configuring a virtual machine (VM) to meet the specific requirements of a project or development task. This includes the installation of necessary software packages, editing configuration files, and setting up network interfaces, among other tasks.

The necessity of provisioning in Vagrant emanates from the need for consistency and reproducibility in development environments. In the absence of provisioning, developers would need to manually configure each VM, a task that is not only time-consuming but also prone to errors. By leveraging provisioning, Vagrant can automate these configurations, ensuring that every member of the development team works within an identical environment. This uniformity significantly reduces the "it works on my machine" syndrome, a common challenge in software development where code runs on the developer's machine but fails in other environments.

Vagrant supports several methods for provisioning environments, including:

- Shell scripts

- Configuration management tools such as Ansible, Chef, and Puppet

Shell scripts offer a straightforward way to execute commands on the VM, making them suitable for simple setup tasks. However, for more complex configurations, configuration management tools provide a more robust solution. These tools not only automate the setup process but also ensure that the environment maintains a desired state through idempotency – a concept we will cover in depth later in this chapter.

One of the distinguishing features of provisioning in Vagrant is the flexibility in defining when and how provisioning occurs. For example, provisioning can be executed:

- At the time of the VM's creation

- Upon request, at any point after the VM has been created

This flexibility is instrumental in maintaining the development environment's integrity over time. It allows for the environment to be updated or modified with minimal effort, ensuring that it remains aligned with the project's evolving requirements.

In summary, provisioning is an indispensable feature in Vagrant that streamlines the setup and maintenance of development environments. By automating the configuration process, it not only saves time but also enhances the reliability and consistency of the environment across different machines. In the coming sections, we will delve deeper into the specifics of various provisioning methods and their practical applications within the Vagrant ecosystem.

3.2   The Role of Provisioning in Automation

Provisioning in the context of automation significantly enhances the efficiency of setting up development environments by automating the repetitive tasks of installing and configuring software. This automation is central to the practice of infrastructure as code (IaC), a key principle in DevOps methodologies, where infrastructure configurations are managed and provisioned through code instead of manual processes.

One of the primary roles of provisioning in automation is to ensure consistency across development, testing, and production environments. This is crucial in minimizing the "it works on my machine" syndrome, a common issue where code behaves differently on different environments due to variations in software configurations. By using provisioning scripts or configuration management tools, environments can be replicated precisely, reducing discrepancies and increasing reliability in deployments.

Furthermore, provisioning automation plays a significant role in the scalability of infrastructure. It allows for the swift setup of new machines to scale an application horizontally, and ensures that each new instance is configured to meet the application's requirements without manual intervention. This scalability is crucial in responding to varying loads, ensuring that applications can handle peak demands efficiently.

Additionally, the automation of provisioning tasks contributes to the reduction of setup and deployment times. By scripting the provisioning process, developers and operations teams can significantly reduce the time it takes to go from a bare-metal server or a clean virtual machine to a fully configured environment ready for development or deployment tasks. This acceleration contributes to faster development cycles and quicker turnaround times for deploying updates or new features.

Moreover, provisioning automation enhances security by ensuring that environments are configured according to best practices and compliance standards. Automating the setup of firewall rules, security patches, and access controls eliminates the risk of human error and ensures that security configurations are consistently applied across all environments.

Consider the use of a simple shell script for provisioning a web server environment:

```
1  #!/bin/bash
2  # Update packages
3  sudo apt-get update
4  # Install Nginx
5  sudo apt-get install -y nginx
6  # Configure Nginx to start on boot
7  sudo systemctl enable nginx
```

In this example, the shell script performs three basic steps: updating the package list, installing Nginx, and configuring Nginx to start on boot. By executing this script as part of the provisioning process in Vagrant, each virtual machine created will have Nginx installed and configured automatically, illustrating how provisioning contributes to the automation of environment setup.

Provisioning plays a critical role in the automation of development environments. It ensures consistency, enhances scalability, reduces setup times, and improves security, aligning with the principles of infrastructure as code and supporting the DevOps practices of continuous integration and continuous deployment.

3.3   Provisioning with Shell Scripts

Provisioning with shell scripts is a straightforward and powerful way to automate the setup of development environments in Vagrant. Shell scripts are essentially sequences of command line instructions executed in order to configure a system. When used in conjunction with Vagrant, these scripts can prepare a virtual machine (VM) by installing software, creating files, and configuring settings immediately after the VM is created.

Creating a Basic Shell Script for Provisioning

To begin, let's create a simple shell script that updates the package lists for upgrades for packages that need upgrading, as well as new packages that have just come to the repositories.

```
1  #!/bin/bash
2  # Update and upgrade the VM
3  sudo apt-get update
4  sudo apt-get upgrade -y
```

In the script above, the 'apt-get update' command fetches the list of available updates from the Internet, and 'apt-get upgrade' applies those updates. The '-y' flag automatically confirms that we want to proceed with the upgrades.

Integrating Shell Scripts with Vagrant

After creating the shell script, the next step is to instruct Vagrant to use this script during the provisioning phase. This is achieved by modifying the Vagrantfile, which configures the behavior of the VM. Insert the following lines into the Vagrantfile to execute the script:

```
1  Vagrant.configure("2") do |config|
2    # Specify the base box
3    config.vm.box = "ubuntu/bionic64"
4
5    # Provisioning with a shell script
6    config.vm.provision "shell", path: "provision.sh"
7  end
```

In this configuration, 'config.vm.provision "shell", path: "provision.sh"' tells Vagrant to execute the shell script named 'provision.sh' found in the same directory as the Vagrantfile.

Advantages of Using Shell Scripts for Provisioning

Using shell scripts for provisioning offers several advantages:

- **Simplicity:** Shell scripts are easy to write and understand, even for those new to automation.

- **Control:** They provide full control over the environment setup, allowing for customized configurations.

- **Portability:** Shell scripts can often be used across various Unix-based systems with little to no modification.

Limitations of Shell Script Provisioning

While shell scripts are beneficial, there are certain limitations:

- **Complexity:** For more complex environments, shell scripts can become difficult to maintain and debug.

- **Idempotency:** Achieving idempotency, the property of provisioning to be safely run multiple times without changing the result beyond the initial application, can be challenging.

- **Platform-Dependence:** Shell scripts may need to be altered for different operating systems or distributions.

Ensuring Idempotency

To mitigate one of the limitations mentioned, here's how to ensure idempotency in a shell provision script:

```
1  #!/bin/bash
2
3  # Install nginx if it's not already installed
4  if ! which nginx > /dev/null; then
5      sudo apt-get update
6      sudo apt-get install -y nginx
7  fi
```

The script uses a conditional to check if nginx is already installed (using 'which nginx'). If not, it proceeds with the update and installation commands. This way, rerunning the provisioning script does not attempt to reinstall nginx if it's already present, demonstrating an approach to idempotency in shell provisioning.

Though simple, provisioning with shell scripts is a powerful approach in Vagrant to automate the configuration of VMs. By understanding the basics of shell scripting and the nuances of integrating them with Vagrant, developers can significantly streamline the process of environment setup. Despite some limitations, the benefits of quick and controlled environment provisioning make shell scripts an essential tool in the developer's toolkit.

3.4   Using Ansible for Provisioning

Provisioning with Ansible is a powerful approach to automate the setup and configuration of Vagrant environments. Ansible is an open-source tool that provides simple yet efficient automation for cross-platform computer support. It uses YAML, a human-readable format, for its playbooks which are the scripts that describe the tasks to be executed.

To utilize Ansible for provisioning in Vagrant, it is essential to have Ansible installed on the host machine. Vagrant communicates with Ansible to trigger the provisioning process on the guest machine. The communication between Vagrant and Ansible is configured within the Vagrantfile, where specific provisioning instructions are defined.

```
1  Vagrant.configure("2") do |config|
2    config.vm.box = "hashicorp/bionic64"
```

```
3   config.vm.provision "ansible" do |ansible|
4     ansible.playbook = "playbook.yml"
5   end
6 end
```

In the example above, a Vagrantfile configuration is shown where Ansible is specified as the provisioner. The `ansible.playbook` specifies the path to the Ansible playbook file, 'playbook.yml', which contains the tasks to be executed.

An Ansible playbook file typically looks like this:

```
1 ---
2 - hosts: all
3   tasks:
4     - name: Update apt repo
5       apt: update_cache=yes
6
7     - name: Install Apache
8       apt: name=apache2 state=present
```

Each task in the playbook is executed in the order they are defined. The first task in the above playbook updates the package manager cache, and the second task installs the Apache web server.

One of the key features of using Ansible for provisioning in Vagrant is idempotency. Ansible plays are idempotent, meaning running the same playbook multiple times will produce the same state on the guest machine without performing unnecessary operations. This feature is particularly useful in development environments, ensuring that provisioning scripts can be run multiple times safely, achieving the same desired configuration without side effects.

- **Flexibility:** Ansible playbooks can be written to provision almost any type of software, from simple applications to complex environments.

- **Simplicity:** The YAML syntax used by Ansible is easy to understand and write, making it accessible to developers and sysadmins alike.

- **Powerful:** Despite its simple syntax, Ansible is powerful enough to handle complex provisioning tasks with ease.

To check the result of a provisioning operation, you can use the Ansible 'debug' module, which can print messages to the console during the execution of a playbook:

```
1    - name: Print debug message
2      debug:
3        msg: "The Apache server is installed."
```

The output of running the playbook will be visible in the Vagrant provisioning process:

```
TASK [Print debug message] ********************************
ok: [default] => {
    "msg": "The Apache server is installed."
}
```

Provisioning with Ansible within Vagrant offers a robust and idempotent method for automating the configuration and setup of virtual environments. By describing the desired state of the system in Ansible playbooks, developers can ensure their development environment remains consistent, portable, and easy to recreate.

3.5   Provisioning with Chef

Chef is a powerful configuration management tool that automates the process of managing infrastructure through code. Unlike simple shell scripts, Chef uses a pure-Ruby, domain-specific language (DSL) for writing system configurations. This section will cover the basics of provisioning Vagrant environments using Chef, ensuring an efficient and repeatable setup process.

To begin, it is fundamental to understand the two primary configurations used by Chef: cookbooks and recipes. A cookbook is the fundamental unit of configuration and policy distribution in Chef, which contains recipes—collections of Ruby code snippets specifying the resources to manage and the order in which these resources are to be applied.

Integrating Chef with Vagrant

Vagrant provides built-in support for provisioning virtual environments with Chef, either through chef_solo for standalone nodes or chef_client for machines that connect to a Chef server. This versatility allows developers to choose the most appropriate provisioning method based on their project's scale and complexity.

Example Vagrantfile configuration for Chef

```
1   Vagrant.configure("2") do |config|
2     config.vm.box = "hashicorp/bionic64"
3
4     # Provisioning with chef_solo
5     config.vm.provision "chef_solo" do |chef|
6       chef.cookbooks_path = ["./cookbooks"]
7       chef.add_recipe("nginx")
8       chef.add_recipe("nodejs")
9       chef.json = {
10        nginx: { worker_processes: 2 },
11        nodejs: { version: '14.x' }
12      }
13    end
14  end
```

In the above Vagrantfile configuration, Vagrant is instructed to provision the virtual machine using chef_solo. The configuration specifies the path to the cookbooks directory relative to the Vagrantfile, and adds recipes for nginx and Node.js to the provisioning process. Additionally, it allows customization of specific software properties through the chef.json attribute, thereby demonstrating the flexibility in configuring environments.

- chef.cookbooks_path defines the path to find cookbooks needed for provisioning.

- chef.add_recipe includes specific recipes from the cookbooks to apply.

- chef.json uses a hash to specify configuration parameters for the recipes.

Best Practices

Leveraging Chef for provisioning in Vagrant presents numerous advantages, including the ability to manage complex configurations with ease and ensuring environment consistency. However, to maximize its benefits, consider the following practices:

- Always use version control for cookbooks and recipes to track changes and facilitate collaboration.

- Leverage community cookbooks whenever possible to avoid reinventing the wheel and to adhere to best practices.

- Test cookbooks locally using tools like Test Kitchen before deploying to avoid environments breaking unexpectedly.

- Ensure idempotency in recipes to guarantee the same outcome regardless of how many times a provisioning operation is executed.

By incorporating these guidelines, developers can streamline their development environment setup with Chef, making it not only highly customisable but also consistent and reproducible across multiple machines.

3.6 Provisioning with Puppet

Provisioning with Puppet in Vagrant is a powerful method for automating the configuration of virtual machines. Puppet is an open-source configuration management tool that allows for the declaration of system state, enforcing the systems to match the declared state. It utilizes a declarative language to specify system configuration, thereby making the entire process reproducible and scalable. This section will cover the essentials of incorporating Puppet as a provisioning tool in Vagrant environments, including basic configurations, setting up a Puppet manifest, and some tips for effectively using Puppet.

Configuring Puppet in Vagrant

To start provisioning your virtual machines with Puppet, you first
need to inform Vagrant about it in your Vagrantfile. This involves
configuring the Vagrantfile to specify Puppet as the chosen
provisioner and pointing it to the appropriate manifest files. A
manifest in Puppet terms is simply a file that describes the desired
state of the system using Puppet's declarative language.

```
1  Vagrant.configure("2") do |config|
2    config.vm.box = "hashicorp/bionic64"
3
4    config.vm.provision "puppet" do |puppet|
5      puppet.manifests_path = "manifests"
6      puppet.manifest_file = "default.pp"
7    end
8  end
```

In the code snippet above, `manifests_path` is set to the directory
where your Puppet manifests are stored, relative to the location of
the Vagrantfile. The `manifest_file` is the entry point for Puppet,
typically set to `default.pp`, but it can be any file within the
`manifests` directory.

Creating a Simple Puppet Manifest

A Puppet manifest file contains the resource declarations.
Resources in Puppet are the basic units for modeling system
configurations, such as packages, services, or files. The following is
a basic Puppet manifest that ensures the Apache web server is
installed and running on a virtual machine:

```
1   class { 'apache':
2     mpm_module => 'prefork',
3   }
4
5   include apache
6
7   apache::vhost { 'example.com':
8     port => '80',
9     docroot => '/var/www/html',
10  }
```

This manifest makes use of the Apache module to manage the

Apache web server. Initially, it declares a class `apache` with the `mpm_module` parameter set to `prefork`. Then, it ensures that the Apache class is included, thus installing Apache and configuring it to use the prefork MPM module. Finally, it configures a virtual host for `example.com`.

Executing Puppet Provisioning

Upon invoking the `vagrant up` command, Vagrant reads the Vagrantfile, starts the virtual machine, and runs the specified provisioning scripts according to the configuration. When Puppet is set as the provisioner, Vagrant triggers Puppet to apply the manifest(s) as outlined in the Vagrantfile configurations.

To view the output of the provisioning process, which can help in debugging, you can use the `vagrant provision` command after the machine is up. This command forces the provisioning scripts to run again, allowing you to see the output in your terminal.

Idioms and Tips for Using Puppet with Vagrant

Here are a few idioms and tips that can be useful when provisioning Vagrant environments with Puppet:

- **Modularity:** Break down your Puppet manifests into modular components for better organization and reusability.

- **Version Control:** Keep your Puppet manifests and modules under version control to track changes and collaborate with others.

- **Testing:** Utilize Puppet's testing tools, like rspec-puppet, to test your manifests and ensure they perform as expected before provisioning.

- **Use of Hiera:** Use Hiera, Puppet's built-in key-value configuration data lookup system, to separate data from your Puppet code. This makes your manifests more reusable and easier to manage.

Incorporating Puppet into Vagrant provides a robust and repeatable mechanism for environment provisioning. By declaring the desired state of the system in Puppet manifests, developers can automate the configuration process, ensure consistency across environments, and significantly decrease the time and effort required to manage virtual machines.

3.7   Inline vs. External Provisioning Scripts

In the provisioning ecosystem of Vagrant, two styles of scripting are prevalent: inline and external provisioning scripts. This distinction is crucial for streamlining the development environment setup and affects how scripts are managed, maintained, and executed within Vagrant.

Inline provisioning scripts are defined directly within the Vagrantfile. This method is particularly useful for succinct scripts or when the provisioning logic is relatively simple. The primary advantage of inline scripts is their directness, allowing developers to quickly comprehend and modify the environment setup without the need to navigate through multiple files. However, this method can lead to cluttered Vagrantfiles if the provisioning logic becomes too complex or extensive. See the following example of an inline provisioning script:

```
1  Vagrant.configure("2") do |config|
2    config.vm.box = "hashicorp/bionic64"
3    config.vm.provision "shell", inline: <<-SHELL
4      apt-get update
5      apt-get install -y apache2
6    SHELL
7  end
```

External provisioning scripts, on the other hand, are separate script files referenced within the Vagrantfile. This approach is suited for complex provisioning tasks or when maintaining scripts in different languages. External scripts enhance the readability and maintainability of the Vagrantfile, particularly for larger projects. The scripts may reside anywhere in the project's directory structure but are commonly placed in a dedicated subdirectory. Below is an example that demonstrates how to reference an external script:

```
1  Vagrant.configure("2") do |config|
2    config.vm.box = "hashicorp/bionic64"
3    config.vm.provision "shell", path: "scripts/install_apache.sh"
4  end
```

There are several considerations to keep in mind when choosing between inline and external provisioning scripts:

- **Project Size and Complexity:** For smaller projects or those with simple provisioning needs, inline scripts may suffice. As the project grows or the provisioning process becomes more intricate, external scripts offer better manageability.

- **Version Control:** External scripts can be easily versioned and tracked using version control systems, offering better insight into changes over time compared to inline scripts embedded within the Vagrantfile.

- **Reusability:** External scripts can be shared and reused across multiple projects, whereas inline scripts are confined to the Vagrantfile in which they are defined.

- **Readability:** Projects with extensive provisioning requirements may benefit from the improved readability that external scripts provide, keeping the Vagrantfile concise and focused solely on Vagrant configuration.

In summary, the choice between inline and external provisioning scripts in Vagrant should be dictated by the specific needs of the project. Inline scripts offer simplicity and immediacy for straightforward tasks, while external scripts provide modularity and manageability, particularly for complex or large-scale provisioning.

3.8   Provisioning Order and Execution

Provisioning in Vagrant not only automates the setup of development environments but also introduces a layer of order and execution logic that is crucial for understanding how these environments are constructed and managed.   This section will dissect the order in which provisioning scripts and tools are executed by Vagrant, and outline the methods available to control and customize this process.

When multiple provisioning scripts are utilized within a single Vagrantfile, Vagrant executes these provisions in the order they are defined. This sequential execution is pivotal, as it allows developers to structure the setup process in a logical sequence, ensuring that dependencies or prerequisites are handled appropriately before moving onto subsequent steps.

For example, consider a scenario where both a shell script and an Ansible playbook are specified for provisioning. The shell script is tasked with updating the package lists and installing Python, which is a prerequisite for Ansible. The Ansible playbook then configures the remaining environment. The corresponding Vagrantfile snippet would appear as follows:

```
1   Vagrant.configure("2") do |config|
2     config.vm.box = "generic/ubuntu2004"
3
4     # Shell script provisioning
5     config.vm.provision "shell", inline: <<-SHELL
6       apt-get update
7       apt-get install -y python
8     SHELL
9
10    # Ansible provisioning
11    config.vm.provision "ansible" do |ansible|
12      ansible.playbook = "playbook.yml"
13    end
```

In this snippet, Vagrant executes the shell provisioner first, followed by the Ansible provisioner. The inline shell script ensures that the necessary package manager updates and installations are performed before Ansible attempts to execute its playbook.

Furthermore, Vagrant offers mechanisms for controlling the execution beyond the simple order of definition. For instance, developers can specify the :run option to control when and how often a provisioner should be executed. By default, provisioners are run every time the vagrant up command is issued. However, setting :run to "once" ensures that the provisioner runs only the first time the virtual machine is created, and not on subsequent vagrant up commands unless explicitly re-provisioned.

```
1  config.vm.provision "shell", run: "once", inline: <<-SHELL
2    echo "This script will only run once."
3  SHELL
```

In addition, Vagrant provides the --provision-with flag with the vagrant up and vagrant reload commands, allowing developers to specify which provisioners to execute. This feature is useful for selectively running certain provisioning scripts without having to execute the entire provisioning sequence.

```
$ vagrant up --provision-with shell
```

This command initiates the Vagrant environment while only running provisions labeled as "shell", ignoring any other provisioners defined in the Vagrantfile.

Lastly, understanding the concept of idempotency, which will be discussed in more detail in a later section, is critical for efficient provisioner execution. Writing provisioners in an idempotent manner ensures that they can be safely run multiple times without causing unintended effects, thus providing a robust mechanism for managing and updating development environments.

The provisioning order and execution strategy within a Vagrant environment are essential for automating and managing development setups. By leveraging the sequence in which provisioners are defined, alongside Vagrant's mechanisms for controlling provisioner execution, developers can achieve a high level of control and customization over their development environments.

3.9   Idempotency in Provisioning

Idempotency, within the context of provisioning in Vagrant, refers to the characteristic of provisioning scripts to achieve the same result regardless of how many times they are executed. This property is crucial for developing automation scripts that can be run multiple times without causing unexpected side effects or errors.

Consider a provisioning script designed to install a software package. If the script lacks idempotency, executing it repeatedly could lead to multiple installations of the same package, resulting in errors or conflicts. Idempotency ensures that if the software is already installed, subsequent executions will not attempt reinstallation, thus avoiding potential issues.

To illustrate the practical implementation of idempotency in provisioning scripts, let's examine a simple shell script designed to install Apache on a Ubuntu virtual machine:

```
1   #!/bin/bash
2
3   if ! dpkg -l | grep -qw apache2; then
4       sudo apt-get update
5       sudo apt-get install -y apache2
6   fi
```

In this script, the if-statement checks if Apache2 is already installed by searching the list of installed packages with dpkg -l and using grep to filter for apache2. The -qw options for grep ensure that it searches quietly and for whole words, respectively. If Apache2 is not found, the script proceeds to update the package lists and install Apache2. This check effectively ensures the idempotency of the script: if Apache2 is already installed, no actions are taken.

It's worth noting that configuration management tools such as Ansible, Chef, and Puppet inherently support idempotency through their design. For example, when using Ansible to manage software installations, the tool's module for package management is designed to check the current state and only apply changes if the target state is not met. Here's an equivalent task in an Ansible playbook for installing Apache2:

```
1  - name Ensure Apache is installed
2    apt
3      name apache2
4      state present
```

The name specifies the package to manage, while the state parameter is set to present, indicating that the package should be installed if it is not already. Ansible's idempotent behavior ensures that if Apache2 is already present, it will not attempt to reinstall it.

The principle of idempotency also extends to the configuration of software and systems. When writing provisioning scripts or using configuration management tools, it's vital to ensure that configurations can be applied multiple times without causing disruption. For instance, repeatedly applying a configuration change should not append or duplicate configuration entries.

In summary, idempotency is a fundamental concept in provisioning that saves time, prevents errors, and ensures the reliability of automation scripts. By designing provisioning processes with idempotency in mind, developers can create more robust, predictable, and maintainable development environments.

3.10 Customizing Provisioning with Environmental Variables

One of the key advantages of using Vagrant for managing development environments is the ability to dynamically configure these environments according to individual project requirements. A crucial aspect of this dynamic configuration revolves around the use of environmental variables. Environmental variables are key-value pairs available to the virtual machine, which can be used to alter the behavior of provisioning scripts or within the applications themselves. In this section, we will discuss how to leverage environmental variables to customize the provisioning process in Vagrant.

The use of environmental variables facilitates a flexible provisioning process, allowing for the configuration to be adjusted without altering the provisioning scripts directly. This is particularly useful when you need to deploy the same application across different environments, such as development, testing, and production, where each environment might require slightly different configurations.

Passing Environmental Variables to Vagrant

To pass environmental variables to Vagrant, you can use the Vagrantfile, which is the main configuration file for Vagrant environments. The Vagrantfile supports embedding Ruby code, which means you can dynamically set environmental variables based on the local environment or any other logic you wish to embed. Below is an example demonstrating how to set environmental variables within the Vagrantfile:

```
1  Vagrant.configure("2") do |config|
2    config.vm.provision "shell", inline: <<-SHELL
3      export DATABASE_URL=postgres://user:password@localhost/dbname
4    SHELL
5  end
```

In this example, an environmental variable named DATABASE_URL is set for the virtual machine, which can be used by provisioning scripts or applications running within the VM to configure database connections.

Accessing Environmental Variables in Provisioning Scripts

Once environmental variables have been set, accessing them within provisioning scripts is straightforward. Whether you are using shell scripts, Ansible playbooks, Chef recipes, or Puppet manifests, environmental variables can be accessed in the usual manner for that environment or technology. Here is an example of accessing an environmental variable in a shell provisioning script:

```
1  #!/bin/bash
2  echo "Using database URL: $DATABASE_URL"
```

This script simply prints the value of the DATABASE_URL environmental variable, showcasing how such variables can be accessed and utilized within provisioning scripts.

Best Practices for Using Environmental Variables

While environmental variables provide a powerful mechanism for customizing provisioning, it is important to follow certain best practices to ensure security and maintainability:

- Avoid hardcoding sensitive information in the Vagrantfile. Consider using a secure storage solution or environment-specific files that are not tracked in version control.

- Use meaningful and consistent names for environmental variables to avoid conflicts and confusion.

- Document the environmental variables used by your Vagrant environment, including their purpose and any default values or required formats.

By adhering to these practices, you can leverage environmental variables to significantly enhance the flexibility and configurability of your Vagrant-managed environments, ensuring that each environment is precisely tailored to meet the requirements of the project at hand.

3.11 Debugging Provisioning Scripts

Debugging provisioning scripts is a critical skill to ensure that the automated environment setup via Vagrant is executed flawlessly. Provisioning scripts, being automated sequences of commands, can sometimes fail due to various reasons such as syntax errors, missing dependencies, or misconfiguration. This section will explore strategies to identify and resolve issues within provisioning scripts.

First, it's important to distinguish between the types of errors that
can occur:

- Syntax errors, which prevent the script from being interpreted
  correctly.

- Runtime errors, which occur during the execution of the script
  due to logic errors, missing files, or external dependencies.

- Configuration errors, which result from incorrect setup or parameters that do not match the expected environment state.

Identifying the type of error is the first step in the debugging process.
Syntax errors are often the easiest to spot and correct, as modern editors provide syntax highlighting and linting capabilities. For shell
scripts, tools like shellcheck can be extremely helpful in identifying
not just syntax issues but also common pitfalls and potential runtime
errors.

To debug runtime errors, the use of verbose output is invaluable.
Vagrant provides a verbose mode that can be enabled by setting the
VAGRANT_LOG environment variable to debug before running the
vagrant provision command. For example:

```
1  $ export VAGRANT_LOG=debug
2  $ vagrant provision
```

This command will produce a detailed log of the provisioning process, allowing you to see each step executed and to pinpoint precisely
where the failure occurs. The verbose output can be quite extensive,
hence searching for keywords such as error, failed, or cannot can
help isolate the issue.

For scripts that involve multiple steps or complex logic, inserting logging statements at various points in the script can help trace the execution flow and identify the stage at which the error occurs. For shell
scripts, simple echo statements can provide insights into the script's
progress:

```
1  echo "Starting package installation"
2  # Package installation commands
3  echo "Package installation complete"
```

92

When encountering configuration errors, it's essential to review the environmental assumptions made by the script. This includes verifying that all required files, directories, and permissions are correctly set up and that external services or dependencies are accessible. Using environmental variables within your Vagrantfile can help manage configurations that might change between executions or environments:

```
1  config.vm.provision "shell", inline: <<-SHELL
2    export API_KEY=${API_KEY}
3    ./configure --with-feature
4  SHELL
```

In this example, the environment variable API_KEY is passed to the provisioning script, allowing for dynamic configuration based on the execution environment.

Lastly, idempotency is a principle that, when applied to provisioning scripts, can simplify debugging by ensuring that script reruns do not introduce additional errors. An idempotent provisioning script can be executed multiple times without changing the final state beyond its initial successful completion. Achieving idempotency typically involves checking the current state before attempting to modify it:

```
1  if [ ! -f /etc/software/configured ]; then
2    echo "Configuring software..."
3    # Configuration commands
4    touch /etc/software/configured
5  fi
```

By following these strategies, you can streamline the debugging process of provisioning scripts, ensuring a more reliable and maintainable environment setup.

3.12   Best Practices for Vagrant Provisioning

Adopting best practices in Vagrant provisioning can significantly enhance the efficiency and reliability of development environments. These practices ensure that provisioning scripts are maintainable, scalable, and can be executed across different environments without modifications. The following guidelines are crucial for achieving optimal results with Vagrant provisioning.

- **Use Version Control:** Keep provisioning scripts under version control to track changes and facilitate collaboration among team members. This approach ensures that any team member can set up their development environment by cloning the repository and running Vagrant up. Additionally, version control facilitates rollback to previous versions of the script if necessary.

- **Employ Idempotent Scripts:** Provisioning scripts should be written in an idempotent manner, meaning that running the script multiple times on the same target environment results in the same configuration without causing errors or unintended side effects. This characteristic is crucial for scripts that may be run multiple times during the development cycle.

```
1   # Example of an idempotent line in a shell provisioning script
2   apt-get install -y apache2 || true
```

- **Modularize Scripts:** Break down the provisioning scripts into modular, reusable components. This practice not only improves readability but also facilitates code reuse across different projects or different parts of the same project.

- **Parameterize Configuration:** Make use of environmental variables to parameterize configuration settings. This allows for flexibility and means that scripts can be customized for different environments without altering the script itself.

```
1   # Example of using environmental variables in a shell script
2   export DATABASE_URL=${DATABASE_URL:-"localhost"}
```

- **Document Scripts:** Comprehensive documentation is essential. Comments within the script should explain the purpose of commands and any dependencies they might have. Documentation external to the code, such as a README file, should describe the overall structure of the provisioning process and any prerequisites for running the scripts.

- **Handle Errors Gracefully:** Scripts should include error handling to manage potential issues during the provisioning process. This practice ensures that the provisioning process is robust and can preemptively address known points of failure.

```
1  # Example of simple error handling in a shell script
2  if ! apt-get update; then
3    echo "Failed to update packages list" >&2
4    exit 1
5  fi
```

- **Optimize Performance:** Consider the performance of provisioning scripts to minimize the time required to provision environments. This can include caching resources, minimizing the size of files to be transferred, and avoiding unnecessary operations.

- **Test Provisioning Scripts:** Regularly test provisioning scripts to validate their functionality across different environments. Consider the use of automated testing tools designed for infrastructure code to ensure that provisioning scripts perform as expected.

- **Secure Sensitive Data:** Avoid hardcoding sensitive information such as passwords or API keys in provisioning scripts. Instead, use environment variables or secure vaults to handle sensitive data securely.

By adhering to these best practices, developers and teams can maximize the benefits of using Vagrant for provisioning development environments, ensuring that these environments are dependable, scalable, and easy to maintain.

Chapter 4

Networking in Vagrant

Networking in Vagrant provides a set of features to configure how the virtual machine managed by Vagrant interacts with the host system, other virtual machines, and the wider network. This functionality is crucial for developing applications that depend on network services or need to be accessible through the network. Vagrant supports several networking options, including port forwarding, private networks, and public networks, each serving different scenarios and requirements. Understanding and correctly implementing these networking features are essential for ensuring the developed applications behave as expected in a networked environment, which this chapter aims to explain and explore in detail.

4.1   The Importance of Networking in Development Environments

Networking is a fundamental aspect of modern computing environments, and its importance is magnified in the context of development environments. This significance can be attributed to several factors, including the need for applications to communicate over networks, access remote resources, and simulate real-world deployment scenarios.

One of the primary reasons networking is essential in development environments is the necessity for applications to communicate with other services. In many cases, applications do not operate in isolation but instead interact with databases, APIs, and other microservices. Configuring networking in development environments allows developers to mimic these interactions closely, ensuring that applications will perform as expected when deployed to production environments.

Access to remote resources is another critical aspect of networking in development environments. Developers often need to fetch dependencies, interact with version control systems, or utilize cloud-based services during the development process. Adequate networking configurations enable these activities, facilitating a smoother and more efficient development workflow.

Furthermore, networking in development environments plays a crucial role in testing. By establishing network configurations that replicate production environments, developers can conduct more accurate and reliable testing. This includes activities such as load testing, where the application's behavior under high traffic conditions is evaluated, and integration testing, where the application's interaction with other services is tested.

To illustrate, consider the configuration of port forwarding in Vagrant, which allows developers to expose a port on the virtual machine to the host machine. This feature is particularly useful for testing web applications, as it enables developers to access the application running inside the virtual machine using a web browser on the host machine.

```
1  Vagrant.configure("2") do |config|
2    config.vm.network "forwarded_port", guest: 80, host: 8080
3  end
```

This code snippet configures port forwarding in Vagrant, mapping port 80 on the guest machine (the virtual machine) to port 8080 on the host machine. As a result, developers can access the web application running on the guest machine by visiting `http://localhost:8080` on the host machine.

```
Accessing the web application:
http://localhost:8080
```

Networking also enables development environments to be more flexible and accessible. For example, configuring a private network in Vagrant allows the virtual machine to communicate with the host machine and other virtual machines on the same network. This setup is beneficial for developing applications that operate in a multi-machine environment.

Networking is a cornerstone of effective development environments, offering the means to simulate real-world scenarios, access remote resources, and interact with other services. Tools like Vagrant provide powerful and flexible networking configurations, empowering developers to create and manage development environments that closely align with production settings, ultimately leading to more reliable and higher-quality software.

4.2 Overview of Networking Options in Vagrant

Vagrant provides a robust set of networking features designed to facilitate various development and testing scenarios by configuring how a virtual machine (VM) interacts with the host machine, other VMs, and the external network. These features are pivotal in simulating real-world environments and ensuring applications developed within Vagrant behave consistently across different environments. Understanding the available networking options and their configurations is crucial for developers to leverage Vagrant effectively. This section will elucidate the three primary networking options supported by Vagrant: Port Forwarding, Private Networks, and Public Networks.

Port Forwarding

Port forwarding is a mechanism that allows external devices to access services on a virtual machine, which would otherwise be isolated and inaccessible. This is achieved by mapping a port on the host machine to a port on the guest machine. For instance, if a web server is running on port 80 in the guest VM, port forwarding can enable accessing this server via a port on the host machine. This setup is particularly useful for development and testing applications running within the VM from the host machine or from other devices in the same network.

To configure port forwarding in Vagrant, the Vagrantfile configuration file is used. A simple example of setting up port forwarding to access a web server running inside a VM is as follows:

```
1  Vagrant.configure("2") do |config|
2    config.vm.box = "hashicorp/precise64"
3    config.vm.network "forwarded_port", guest: 80, host: 8080
4  end
```

In the above example, requests made to port 8080 on the host machine are forwarded to port 80 on the guest VM.

Private Networks

Private networks allow the host machine and the VM to communicate over a network that is isolated from the external world. This is useful for scenarios where multiple VMs need to communicate with each other or with the host machine without exposing services to the public internet. Vagrant supports the creation of private networks with flexible configuration options, including the ability to specify static IP addresses.

To create a private network in Vagrant, the Vagrantfile must be edited as demonstrated below:

```
1  Vagrant.configure("2") do |config|
2    config.vm.box = "hashicorp/precise64"
3    config.vm.network "private_network", ip: "192.168.56.101"
4  end
```

The above configuration assigns the static IP 192.168.56.101 to the VM, allowing it to communicate with the host machine through this address.

Public Networks

Public networks bridge the VM directly onto the network to which the host machine is connected, allowing the VM to obtain an IP address within the same subnet as the host. This mode effectively treats the VM as another physical device on the network, making it reachable by other devices within the same network without any special configuration. Public networking is suitable for scenarios where the VM needs to act as a server or be a part of a larger network infrastructure.

Configuring a VM to use a public network in Vagrant is accomplished by adding a similar line to the Vagrantfile, as shown below:

```
1  Vagrant.configure("2") do |config|
2    config.vm.box = "hashicorp/precise64"
3    config.vm.network "public_network"
4  end
```

Depending on the network setup and requirements, further configuration may be necessary for public networks, such as specifying a particular bridge interface.

In summary, Vagrant's networking capabilities are designed to offer flexibility and mimic real-world deployment scenarios. By understanding and utilizing these networking options, developers can ensure their applications are well-tested and behave consistently across different environments.

4.3 Port Forwarding: Concepts and Configuration

Port forwarding, a pivotal networking feature in Vagrant, enables external users or systems to access services on a virtual machine

(VM) through specific ports on the host machine. This approach helps in circumventing the issue where the VM is in a network that is unreachable by the user's device. With port forwarding, a network request on a given port on the host is forwarded to a specified port on the guest VM, effectively making the service on the VM accessible.

Configuring port forwarding in Vagrant is straightforward, facilitated by the Vagrantfile – a primary configuration file that defines the VM's settings. To set up port forwarding, one must specify the guest and host ports within the Vagrantfile. Here's how:

```
1   Vagrant.configure("2") do |config|
2     config.vm.network "forwarded_port", guest: 80, host: 8080
3   end
```

In the above code snippet, the configuration directive config.vm.network is used to define a port forwarding rule. The parameters guest: 80 and host: 8080 imply that any network requests on port 8080 on the host will be forwarded to port 80 on the guest VM. This is particularly useful for web development, allowing developers to access a web server running inside the VM by navigating to localhost:8080 on their browser.

Multiple port forwarding rules can be defined within the same Vagrantfile, as demonstrated below:

```
1   Vagrant.configure("2") do |config|
2     config.vm.network "forwarded_port", guest: 80, host: 8080
3     config.vm.network "forwarded_port", guest: 443, host: 8443
4   end
```

This configuration forwards HTTPS traffic from port 8443 on the host to port 443 on the guest, in addition to the HTTP forwarding defined previously.

After configuring port forwarding in the Vagrantfile, the changes need to be applied. This is done by either starting the VM if it is not already running with vagrant up or by reloading the VM configuration with vagrant reload if the VM is already running. The command to apply the changes is as follows:

```
1   vagrant reload
```

The following output is expected upon a successful reload, indicating that the port forwarding is in effect:

```
==> default: Forwarding ports...
    default: 80 (guest) => 8080 (host) (adapter 1)
    default: 443 (guest) => 8443 (host) (adapter 1)
```

It is important to note that the host ports specified in forwarding rules must be available and not in use by any other service. If a port is already in use, Vagrant will display an error message, prompting the user to choose a different host port.

In summary, port forwarding in Vagrant is an essential tool for developers, enabling them to access services and applications running within a VM from their host machine. Properly configuring and managing port forwarding rules in the Vagrantfile adds versatility to the development environment, ensuring seamless access to the necessary services during the development process.

4.4 Setting Up a Private Network

Configuring a private network in Vagrant allows virtual machines (VMs) to communicate with each other in isolation from external networks. This is particularly beneficial for testing inter-VM communication without exposing the network setup to the broader network. A private network in Vagrant can either assign fixed IP addresses to each VM or rely on a DHCP server to dynamically allocate IPs.

Before delving into the configuration process, it is vital to understand the key benefits of utilizing a private network in development environments. Firstly, it enhances security by isolating the network traffic among VMs from the external network. Secondly, it offers a controlled environment for application testing, simulating a production-like network topology. Finally, it aids in the management of network configurations, ensuring consistency across development, testing, and production environments.

Vagrantfile Configuration for Private Networks

To configure a private network in Vagrant, adjustments are made to the `Vagrantfile`. This file contains the configuration specifics for VMs managed by Vagrant. Herein, an IP address is specified for the private network interface of the VM. Alternatively, DHCP can be enabled to automatically assign IP addresses.

Assigning a Fixed IP

To assign a fixed IP address to a VM, the following configuration is applied:

```
Vagrant.configure("2") do |config|
  config.vm.network "private_network", ip: "192.168.50.4"
end
```

In this configuration, the `192.168.50.4` IP address is statically assigned to the VM's private network interface. It is crucial to ensure that the IP address provided does not conflict with existing devices on the network.

Enabling DHCP

To enable DHCP, allowing automatic IP address assignment, the configuration is as follows:

```
Vagrant.configure("2") do |config|
  config.vm.network "private_network", type: "dhcp"
end
```

This setup instructs Vagrant to request an IP address from the DHCP server for the VM's private network interface. It's a practical approach for environments where IP address management is dynamic, and manual assignment is impractical.

Verifying the Configuration

After configuring the private network, the setup can be verified by accessing the VM through SSH and checking the network interface's IP address. The verification process involves the following steps:

```
1  vagrant ssh
2  ip addr show
```

This command displays the network configurations of the VM, including the IP addresses assigned to each network interface. Verify that the private network interface has the expected IP address, whether statically assigned or dynamically allocated through DHCP.

Troubleshooting

Issues can arise in configuring private networks, such as IP conflicts or inability to communicate between VMs. To troubleshoot, ensure the following:

- The IP address range does not conflict with the host's network or other VMs.

- Networking services (e.g., firewalls or network address translation) on the host are correctly configured to allow VM communication.

- The Vagrant and VirtualBox (or another provider) software versions are up-to-date to avoid compatibility issues.

Proper configuration and verification of private networks in Vagrant are essential steps in setting up a development environment that closely mimics production systems. By assigning IP addresses manually or via DHCP, developers have the flexibility to create isolated and secure network environments tailored to their application's needs. Furthermore, understanding and troubleshooting common networking issues can enhance the stability and reliability of these environments.

4.5   Configuring a Public Network

Configuring a public network in Vagrant is essential for scenarios where the virtual machine (VM) needs to be accessible by other devices on the same network, or even from the internet. This level of network access can be indispensable for testing how a developed application responds to real-world requests or for staging versions of web applications before they are deployed to a production environment.

To configure a public network, the Vagrantfile must be edited to include specific networking configurations. The Vagrantfile is a Ruby file used to configure Vagrant environments on a per-project basis.

```
1  Vagrant.configure("2") do |config|
2    config.vm.network "public_network"
3  end
```

This code snippet adds a public network interface to the VM managed by Vagrant. Upon executing vagrant up, Vagrant will attempt to configure this network interface by bridging it with an available network interface on the host machine. This setup allows the VM to obtain an IP address that can be accessible from other machines on the same network.

It is possible to specify the bridge interface manually if the host machine has multiple network interfaces. This is accomplished by adding an additional option to the config.vm.network line in the Vagrantfile:

```
1  Vagrant.configure("2") do |config|
2    config.vm.network "public_network", bridge: "en0: Wi-Fi (AirPort)"
3  end
```

In this example, "en0: Wi-Fi (AirPort)" is the name of the network interface on a macOS computer. Users should replace this with the relevant network interface name on their own host machine, which may vary depending on the operating system and the network configuration.

Furthermore, you can assign a static IP to the VM to ensure it obtains the same IP address each time it boots. This facilitates reliable access to the VM, especially important when working in teams or when configuring DNS records for web applications.

```
1  Vagrant.configure("2") do |config|
2    config.vm.network "public_network", ip: "192.168.1.100"
3  end
```

Specifying an IP address, however, requires ensuring the chosen IP does not conflict with other devices on the network. It is advisable to consult with network administrators or to refer to the DHCP server configuration to determine a safe range of IP addresses.

After making these changes to the Vagrantfile, running vagrant reload or vagrant up will apply the new network configuration. One can verify the network interface configuration within the VM using network command-line tools such as ifconfig or ip addr.

```
$ ifconfig eth1
eth1      Link encap:Ethernet  HWaddr 08:00:27:4e:8b:76
          inet addr:192.168.1.100  Bcast:192.168.1.255  Mask:255.255.255.0
          ...
```

In this output, eth1 represents the network interface configured by Vagrant for the public network, showing that the VM has successfully obtained the IP address 192.168.1.100.

It is crucial to consider network security when exposing VMs to a public network. Firewall rules and security groups should be meticulously configured to expose only the necessary ports and services to minimize the attack surface.

To summarize, configuring a public network in Vagrant involves editing the Vagrantfile to specify the desired networking options, including the choice of bridging an interface, assigning a static IP, and ensuring the security of the networked environment. Properly understanding and implementing these configurations are vital for the development and testing of applications in a networked setting.

4.6   Networking Between Host and Guest Machines

In this section, we will discuss the mechanisms and procedures through which Vagrant facilitates networking between the host and guest machines, enabling direct communication pivotal for various developmental and testing activities.

Vagrant's networking capabilities provide seamless interaction between the host and guest environments.   This interaction is fundamentally important for tasks like API testing, web server configuration, and database access from the host machine.

To begin, let's understand how Vagrant approaches networking between the host and guest machines. There are mainly two ways to configure this:

- Port Forwarding

- Private Network

Port Forwarding is primarily used to expose guest services on the host's network interfaces. It maps a port on the host to a port on the guest, allowing network traffic to be directed to the specified port on the host and then forwarded to the guest machine.

An example configuration in Vagrantfile for port forwarding would be:

```
Vagrant.configure("2") do |config|
   config.vm.network "forwarded_port", guest: 80, host: 8080
end
```

This setting forwards traffic from port 8080 on the host to port 80 on the guest, typically used for accessing a web server running inside the guest machine from the host's web browser.

Private Network, on the other hand, allows the virtual machine to receive an IP address that is reachable from the host. This is akin to the guest and host machines being on the same physical network.

108

A sample configuration for setting up a private network in Vagrant
would be:

```
1  Vagrant.configure("2") do |config|
2      config.vm.network "private_network", type: "dhcp"
3  end
```

With this configuration, the guest machine is assigned an IP address
dynamically via DHCP. Alternatively, a static IP can be assigned as
follows:

```
1  Vagrant.configure("2") do |config|
2      config.vm.network "private_network", ip: "192.168.33.10"
3  end
```

This setup facilitates direct access to the guest machine from the
host, using the designated IP address, for scenarios that require
more than just port forwarding, such as multi-machine clusters
where each guest would have a unique IP address within the
private network.

For verifying the connectivity from the host to the guest, one can use
the ping command:

```
$ ping 192.168.33.10
```

If the network configuration is correct, the ping command should
show responses from the specified IP address, indicating successful
communication between the host and guest machines.

Implementing effective networking between host and guest not
only simplifies development and testing but also enhances the
capacity for automation and orchestration in multi-machine
Vagrant environments. It's crucial for the development team to
familiarize themselves with these networking options to tailor the
development environment to the project's needs closely.

In subsequent sections, we will explore more about managing IP addresses and setting up stable environments using static IPs, which
further sophisticate the networking capabilities of Vagrant environments.

4.7   Managing IP Addresses in Vagrant

Managing IP addresses in Vagrant is a critical aspect of setting up and maintaining a development environment that relies on networking. This section will discuss the configuration of static and dynamic IP addresses within Vagrant environments, highlighting the significance of each approach in different scenarios.

For configuring network settings, Vagrant provides an intuitive interface via the Vagrantfile. This configuration file is a primary resource for managing the settings of your Vagrant machines, including networking configurations.

Using Static IPs for Stable Environments

Static IP addresses are often used when a stable network configuration is essential. Assigning a static IP to a Vagrant box ensures that the IP address remains the same each time the Vagrant machine is started. This stability is particularly useful for environments where the machine needs to be consistently accessible at the same address for services like continuous integration servers, or for configurations where other machines depend on the IP address of your Vagrant machine.

To configure a static IP in Vagrant, modify the Vagrantfile with the following configuration, using the `config.vm.network` directive:

```
1  Vagrant.configure("2") do |config|
2    config.vm.box = "hashicorp/bionic64"
3    config.vm.network "private_network", ip: "192.168.33.10"
4  end
```

In this example, the Vagrant machine is assigned a static IP address of "192.168.33.10". This IP address should be chosen carefully to avoid conflicts with other devices on the network.

Configuring Dynamic IP Addresses

While static IP assignments are suitable for stable environments, dynamic IP configurations can be advantageous for temporary development environments or when the network's structure is fluid. Dynamic IPs are allocated each time the Vagrant machine is started, usually using DHCP.

Configuring a dynamic IP in Vagrant does not require specifying an IP address. Instead, use the type: "dhcp" option in the Vagrantfile:

```
Vagrant.configure("2") do |config|
  config.vm.box = "hashicorp/bionic64"
  config.vm.network "private_network", type: "dhcp"
end
```

This configuration instructs Vagrant to request an IP address from the DHCP server present in your network. While this approach offers flexibility, it may introduce unpredictability in accessing your Vagrant machine due to the changing IP address.

Accessing Assigned IP Addresses

After configuring the network and starting your Vagrant environment, you may need to access the assigned IP address. Vagrant provides a simple command to retrieve the current network configuration:

```
$ vagrant ssh -c "hostname -I"
```

This command logs into the Vagrant machine and executes the hostname -I command, which displays the machine's IP addresses. Note that in the case of dynamic IP configuration, the IP address may change with each restart of the Vagrant machine.

Successfully managing IP addresses in Vagrant environments is crucial for ensuring that your development environment is properly networked. While static IPs provide stability and predictability, dynamic IPs offer flexibility. The choice between static and dynamic IP configurations depends on the specific needs of your project and your network environment.

4.8   Using Static IPs for Stable Environments

In this section, we will discuss the application and benefits of using static IPs within Vagrant environments. A static IP address remains constant throughout each session and upon each boot of the Vagrant environment, in contrast to dynamic IPs which can change each time the network interface asks the DHCP (Dynamic Host Configuration Protocol) server for an IP address. This stability plays a pivotal role in development environments, especially when these environments are accessed or interacted with by other machines or services.

Configuration of Static IPs

To configure a static IP, modifications must be made to the Vagrantfile, which acts as the configuration file for individual Vagrant machines. Within the Vagrantfile, you can specify a static IP for a private network. Here is an example of how to set up a static IP:

Configuring a Static IP in Vagrantfile

```
1  Vagrant.configure("2") do |config|
2      config.vm.network "private_network", ip: "192.168.50.4"
3  end
```

After adding the above code to your Vagrantfile, the virtual machine will always use the static IP 192.168.50.4 when it is created or restarted. Remember to replace 192.168.50.4 with an IP address that suits your network's addressing scheme and doesn't conflict with other devices.

Benefits of Using Static IPs

Various benefits are associated with employing static IPs in development environments, including:

- **Simplified Access**: With a static IP, developers can consistently access the virtual machine or service running within Vagrant

112

without the need to reconfigure clients or scripts that interact with it due to IP changes.

- **Enhanced Integration**: Continuous Integration (CI) and Continuous Deployment (CD) pipelines can reliably interact with known, stable endpoints. This stability is especially advantageous when the Vagrant machine offers services consumed by other applications or services.

- **Network Simplification**: Managing network resources and policies becomes easier when IPs do not change. Firewall rules, access control lists, and DNS configurations can be set up once and require less frequent updates.

Considerations When Using Static IPs

While the use of static IPs provides numerous benefits, there are several important considerations to keep in mind:

- Ensure that the chosen static IP does not conflict with other devices on the same network. IP conflicts can lead to unpredictable behavior and difficulty in accessing the Vagrant environment or other network resources.

- Be mindful of the network's IP addressing scheme and potential restrictions. It is essential to choose an IP address that conforms to the network's architectural guidelines and available address space.

- Regularly review network policies and configurations to ensure they continue to meet security and access requirements for the static IP-addressed resources.

Static IPs, when used wisely within Vagrant environments, offer a level of stability and predictability that can vastly improve development workflows, integration efforts, and overall network management. By following the outlined steps for configuration and adhering to the network's guidelines and best practices, developers can harness the full potential of static IPs to create efficient and reliable development environments.

4.9   Accessing the Vagrant Environment from External Machines

Accessing the Vagrant environment from external machines is a pivotal step in validating the functionality and accessibility of applications under development. This process allows developers, testers, or clients to interact with the software as if it were deployed in a real-world scenario. The ability to do so hinges on properly configuring the network settings of the Vagrant environment. In this section, we will discuss the mechanisms of enabling external access, focusing on configuring public networks and port forwarding.

Public networks in Vagrant are configured in such a way that the virtual machine (VM) obtains an IP address from the same network the host is connected to. This setup allows other devices on the same network to communicate with the VM directly. To configure a public network, one must edit the Vagrantfile to include a public network configuration block. The following example demonstrates how to configure a Vagrant-managed VM to use a public network:

```
1  Vagrant.configure("2") do |config|
2    config.vm.network "public_network"
3  end
```

This configuration informs Vagrant to attach the VM to the public network. By default, Vagrant will use DHCP to assign an IP address to the VM. It is possible to assign a static IP address to ensure the address remains constant, which is particularly useful for long-term projects.

```
1  Vagrant.configure("2") do |config|
2    config.vm.network "public_network", ip: "192.168.1.100"
3  end
```

Upon applying either of the above configurations, the Vagrant environment must be reloaded for the changes to take effect, accomplished by using the `vagrant reload` command.

For scenarios where configuring a public network is not viable, port forwarding offers an alternative method for allowing external access to applications running within a Vagrant VM. This method forwards requests from a specific port on the host machine to a port on the guest machine. The following configuration snippet showcases how to forward port 8080 on the host to port 80 on the guest:

```
1  Vagrant.configure("2") do |config|
2    config.vm.network "forwarded_port", guest: 80, host: 8080
3  end
```

This set up enables accessing the web application running inside the Vagrant VM by navigating to `http://localhost:8080` on the host machine or any external machine that can route to the host machine's IP address.

After configuring either public networks or port forwarding in the Vagrantfile, it's imperative to verify connectivity from external machines. For devices within the same network, this typically involves simply entering the host machine's IP address and the forwarded port into a web browser. For machines outside the network, additional networking configurations, such as NAT (Network Address Translation) configuration on routers or firewalls, may be necessary.

Accessing the Vagrant environment from external machines is essential for testing and demonstration purposes. By correctly configuring public networks or utilizing port forwarding, developers can ensure their applications are accessible and functional from any location, mirroring production environments more closely.

4.10 Troubleshooting Common Networking Issues

Troubleshooting networking issues in Vagrant environments can be a daunting task, due to the complexity of network configurations and the variety of potential problems that can arise. This section will delve into solutions for common issues, such as connectivity problems, port collisions, and incorrect IP configurations, aiming to provide a comprehensive guide to resolving such issues promptly and efficiently.

Connectivity Issues

One of the most frequent challenges encountered is the lack of connectivity between the host and the guest machine or between multiple VMs. This problem often manifests as an inability to ping the guest machine or access its services from the host. The following steps can help diagnose and resolve connectivity issues:

- Verify the network configuration in the Vagrantfile. Ensure that the network type (private, public, or forwarded port) matches the intended use case.

- Ensure that the firewall on the host or guest machine is not blocking connections. Temporarily disabling the firewall can help determine if it is the cause of the connectivity issues.

- Use the `vagrant reload` command to restart the virtual machine and apply any changes to the network configuration.

- Check the network adapter settings in the virtual machine provider's GUI (e.g., VirtualBox or VMware) to ensure they align with the network settings specified in the Vagrantfile.

Port Forwarding Issues

Port forwarding is essential for accessing services on the guest machine by mapping its ports to the host machine's ports. Common issues with port forwarding include port collisions and connection timeouts. To troubleshoot port forwarding issues:

- Confirm that the forwarded port on the host machine is not being used by another application. Use the command `netstat`

116

`-tuln` on Linux/Unix or `netstat -aon` on Windows to list occupied ports.

- Ensure that the port numbers specified in the Vagrantfile's port forwarding configuration do not conflict with other VMs or services.

- If a port collision is detected, choose an alternate port number for the forwarding rule in the Vagrantfile, and apply the changes by running `vagrant reload`.

Incorrect IP Configuration

For private or public networks, an incorrect IP configuration can lead to a virtual machine being unreachable. This may occur if the IP address assigned to the VM conflicts with another device on the network or if the subnet does not match the network's configuration. To resolve issues related to incorrect IP configurations:

- Ensure that the IP address specified in the Vagrantfile for the VM is within the correct subnet range and does not conflict with existing devices on the network.

- For static IP configurations, verify that the IP address is not assigned via DHCP to another device.

- Consider using DHCP for dynamic IP assignment if static IPs are not strictly required, to avoid manual IP conflict resolution.

Debugging with Vagrant Commands

Vagrant provides several command-line tools for diagnosing and fixing network-related issues:

```
1   vagrant status # Check the status of the VMs
2   vagrant up --debug # Start the VM with debugging enabled for detailed error
        output
3   vagrant provision # Reapply configuration without restarting the VM
4   vagrant ssh-config # Display SSH connection details for debugging SSH issues
```

In summary, networking issues in Vagrant environments are typically related to connectivity, port forwarding, or IP configuration problems. By systematically checking configurations, ensuring there are no conflicts or misconfigurations, and utilizing Vagrant's built-in commands for diagnostics, most networking issues can be resolved efficiently. Additionally, consulting the documentation of the specific virtual machine provider (e.g., VirtualBox, VMware) for provider-specific networking issues and configurations is advisable.

4.11   Security Considerations for Vagrant Networking

When working with networking in Vagrant, security should never be an afterthought. The configuration of network settings in a development environment can inadvertently expose the system to security threats, ranging from unauthorized data access to the exploitation of vulnerabilities within the system. This section delineates the security considerations that must be accounted for when configuring networking within a Vagrant environment.

One critical aspect to consider is the setting up of port forwarding. By default, Vagrant maps or forwards ports from the guest machine to the host machine to allow network services such as web servers to be accessible from the host. However, this can expose services intended only for development purposes to the outside world.

```
1   Vagrant.configure("2") do |config|
2     config.vm.network "forwarded_port", guest: 80, host: 8080
3   end
```

While the code snippet above is a typical configuration for port forwarding, it's essential to ensure that the host ports exposed do not conflict with existing services and are not accessible by unauthorized users. This can be managed by configuring the host's firewall properly or using more specific Vagrant plugins to handle security.

Implementing private networks in Vagrant offers a safer alternative, allowing the host and guest machines to communicate with each other in a segregated network. This method can significantly reduce the risk of external attacks but requires careful configuration to avoid creating vulnerabilities.

```
1  Vagrant.configure("2") do |config|
2    config.vm.network "private_network", type: "dhcp"
3  end
```

The configuration above establishes a DHCP-based private network, which is isolated from the public internet and other devices on the host's network. Nevertheless, practitioners must remain vigilant of the security implications within this isolated network, such as ensuring that the Vagrant box itself does not contain malicious code or vulnerabilities.

Public networks in Vagrant pose the most significant security risk. Configuring a public network allows the guest machine to communicate directly with the outside world, akin to any physical device on the network.

```
1  Vagrant.configure("2") do |config|
2    config.vm.network "public_network"
3  end
```

This setup should be used sparingly and always with stringent security measures in place, such as advanced firewall configurations and rigorous network monitoring, to mitigate potential threats.

Another imperative security consideration is the management of IP addresses. Whether using static or dynamic IP configurations, understanding the network layout and ensuring that IP addresses are not conflicting or exposing the Vagrant environment to security risks is crucial.

Moreover, when accessing the Vagrant environment from external machines, it's paramount to employ secure access methods, such as SSH with strong authentication mechanisms and encrypted traffic, to protect against data interception and unauthorized access.

```
vagrant ssh
```

The command above initiates an SSH session to the Vagrant guest

119

machine, leveraging Vagrant's built-in secure configuration. However, modifying the default SSH settings to further harden security can be beneficial, like disabling password-based login in favor of key-based authentication.

In summary, security considerations in Vagrant networking are multifaceted and require diligent attention to detail during configuration. Safe practices include limiting port forwarding, leveraging private networks, being cautious with public network configurations, carefully assigning and managing IP addresses, and securing access methods. By adhering to these guidelines, developers can create Vagrant environments that are not only functional and efficient but also secure.

4.12   Advanced   Networking: Bridged Adapters and DHCP

Advanced networking configurations in Vagrant, such as the use of bridged adapters and the Dynamic Host Configuration Protocol (DHCP), are essential for creating sophisticated and flexible development environments. This section discusses these two advanced features, their applications, and the process of configuring them in a Vagrant environment.

Bridged Adapters

Bridged networking connects a virtual machine directly to a network using the host machine's physical network adapter. In this mode, the virtual machine appears as a separate device on the network, obtaining an IP address from the network's DHCP server, just like any other physical machine on the network.

Configuration:

To configure a bridged adapter in Vagrant, modify the Vagrantfile to include the necessary networking option. Here is an example:

```
1  config.vm.network "public_network", use_dhcp_assigned_default_route: true
```

In this configuration, Vagrant is instructed to create a public network interface, where the virtual machine will use DHCP to obtain an IP address. The `use_dhcp_assigned_default_route: true` option allows the virtual machine to communicate with the outside network through the host machine's network adapter.

Dynamic Host Configuration Protocol (DHCP)

DHCP is a network management protocol used to automatically assign IP addresses and other network configuration parameters to devices on a network. When using Vagrant, DHCP can facilitate the automatic assignment of IP addresses to virtual machines, reducing the need for manual configuration and ensuring that IP addresses are managed efficiently.

Configuring DHCP:

Vagrant typically manages DHCP configurations internally but allows some level of customization for specific networking needs. For instance, if you need to specify a range of IP addresses for your Vagrant machines, you can do so by editing the configuration of the DHCP server on the host machine or within Vagrant's networking settings.

Example of specifying a range of IP addresses:

```
1  config.vm.network "private_network", type: "dhcp"
```

This line in the Vagrantfile configures a private network where the virtual machine will receive an IP address dynamically allocated by DHCP. No static IP needs to be specified, making this an advantageous option for environments where IP management is handled externally.

Benefits:

The use of bridged adapters and DHCP in Vagrant offers several benefits:

- Seamless integration of virtual machines into existing networks, making them indistinguishable from physical machines on the network.

- Dynamic allocation and management of IP addresses, reducing the need for manual network configuration.

- Enhanced network communication capabilities between the host and guest machines, external devices, and the Internet.

However, it's important to understand the security implications of bridged networking, as it exposes virtual machines to the same network vulnerabilities as physical machines. Proper security measures, such as firewalls and access controls, should be implemented to protect the development environment.

Bridged adapters and DHCP configuration in Vagrant offer powerful options for advanced networking needs. By understanding and correctly implementing these features, developers can create highly accessible and flexible development environments that mimic production environments closely.

Chapter 5

Multi-Machine Environments

Multi-Machine Environments in Vagrant allow users to define and manage multiple virtual machines within a single Vagrantfile, offering a way to simulate a network of machines or set up different roles within a development project. This capability is crucial for projects that require different services to be separated on different VMs or for creating more complex test environments that more accurately reflect production setups. By orchestrating multiple machines, developers can ensure their applications work seamlessly in distributed architectures. This chapter will cover the configuration, management, and practical use cases of multi-machine setups in Vagrant, providing readers with the knowledge to effectively manage complex environments.

5.1   Introduction   to   Multi-Machine Environments

Let's start with the foundation of multi-machine environments in Vagrant, which empower users to orchestrate and manage the interaction of multiple virtual machines (VMs) within a single Vagrant environment. This is a paradigm shift from the traditional use of Vagrant, which often focuses on a single VM to mirror a development environment. The multi-machine feature extends this capability, allowing for the simulation of more complex systems that mirror production environments more closely or to segregate different components of a development project across several VMs for isolation or role-specific configuration.

In essence, a multi-machine setup in Vagrant enables the definition, configuration, and control of multiple VMs through a single `Vagrantfile`.   This `Vagrantfile` acts as the blueprint for the environment, detailing the configurations for each VM. The ability to define multiple machines in this manner simplifies the process of setting up, for instance, a multi-tier application, where you might have a web server running on one VM, a database server on another, and perhaps a caching layer on a third.

One of the significant advantages of utilizing multi-machine environments is the ease with which developers can mimic distributed systems or architectures. This is particularly useful for testing the interaction between different components of an application in a controlled and replicable manner. Such setups can range from simple configurations, where two VMs are networked together, to more complex scenarios involving several machines with varying roles and network configurations.

Networking between these machines is a pivotal aspect of multi-machine environments. Vagrant provides several networking options to facilitate communication between the VMs. These can be configured to simulate real-world network setups, including private networks for inter-VM communication, and public networks that expose services to the host system or beyond.

Provisioning tools play a vital role in the setup of multi-machine environments, allowing for automated setup of software and configurations across all VMs according to their roles. Whether using shell scripts, Ansible, Chef, or Puppet, provisioning ensures that each VM is appropriately configured for its intended purpose without manual intervention.

Given the complexity and potential of multi-machine environments, there are several factors to consider in their setup and management. These range from how to effectively synchronize folders across VMs, to managing dependencies between machines, to allocating resources so that the host system remains performant.

Throughout this chapter, the intricacies of configuring, managing, and utilizing multi-machine environments in Vagrant will be explored. These discussions will serve to equip developers with the knowledge and skills necessary to leverage Vagrant's full potential in simulating and managing distributed architectures or complex systems within their development workflows.

5.2 Defining Multiple Machines in a Vagrantfile

In a multi-machine Vagrant environment, the Vagrantfile serves as a central blueprint for configuring and managing all virtual machines (VMs) involved in the setup. To begin, let us delve into the basics of defining multiple machines within this Vagrantfile.

The primary mechanism for specifying multiple VMs in a single Vagrantfile is through the use of the *config.vm.define* method. This method allows you to create a unique identifier for each VM and pass a block of configuration settings specific to that machine.

Consider the following example where we define two machines: a web server and a database server.

```
1  Vagrant.configure("2") do |config|
2
3    config.vm.define "web" do |web|
4      web.vm.box = "ubuntu/bionic64"
```

```
5       web.vm.hostname = "web-server"
6       web.vm.network "private_network", type: "dhcp"
7     end
8
9     config.vm.define "db" do |db|
10      db.vm.box = "ubuntu/bionic64"
11      db.vm.hostname = "db-server"
12      db.vm.network "private_network", type: "dhcp"
13    end
14
15  end
```

In the above `Vagrantfile`, two VMs are defined: `web` and `db`. Each VM is based on the Ubuntu 18.04 LTS (Bionic Beaver) 64-bit box. Additionally, both VMs are configured to use a private network with Dynamic Host Configuration Protocol (DHCP) to automatically assign IP addresses.

It's crucial to understand the structure of the configuration block for each VM:

- `config.vm.define` specifies the name of the VM, which can later be used for referencing the VM through Vagrant commands.

- Inside the block passed to `config.vm.define`, the VM is configured using methods such as `vm.box` for setting the base image, `vm.hostname` for naming the VM within the network, and `vm.network` for networking configurations.

Beyond basic configuration, you might need to allocate resources such as CPU and memory to your VMs. This is achieved by configuring the provider-specific settings within the same block. For example, to set the number of CPUs and the amount of memory for the web server VM, you might add the following configuration:

```
1   web.vm.provider "virtualbox" do |vb|
2     vb.memory = "1024"
3     vb.cpus = 2
4   end
```

Here, the `web.vm.provider` block allows us to specify settings related to VirtualBox, the underlying provider. In this case, we're setting the web server VM to use 1024 MB of RAM and 2 CPUs.

To validate the configuration of your multi-machine environment, the vagrant status command can be utilized. This command provides a list of all VMs defined in the Vagrantfile and their current states. For instance, executing vagrant status might yield the following output:

```
Current machine states:

web                     not created (virtualbox)
db                      not created (virtualbox)

This environment represents multiple VMs. The VMs are all listed
above with their current state. For more information about a specific
VM, run `vagrant status NAME`.
```

This concise overview elucidates the pivotal steps and considerations in defining multiple machines within a Vagrantfile. By leveraging the config.vm.define method and delineating configuration blocks for each VM, you can facilely orchestrate a multi-machine Vagrant setup tailored to your project's requirements.

5.3   Networking Between Multiple VMs

Networking between multiple VMs in a Vagrant environment is essential for simulating real-world scenarios where services communicate with each other over a network. This section focuses on the configuration options available for networking in a multi-machine Vagrant setup, emphasizing the importance of understanding networking modes—private network, public network, and forwarded ports—to ensure effective communication between virtual machines.

Private Network

A private network is often used for internal communication between VMs on the same Vagrant environment. This network is isolated from the host machine and the internet, making it suitable for sensitive applications that should not be exposed publicly.

To configure a private network, you can add a private network interface to your Vagrantfile:

```
1  Vagrant.configure("2") do |config|
2    config.vm.define "machine1" do |machine1|
3      machine1.vm.network "private_network", type: "dhcp"
4    end
5    config.vm.define "machine2" do |machine2|
6      machine2.vm.network "private_network", type: "dhcp"
7    end
8  end
```

This configuration assigns an IP address to each machine via DHCP. Alternatively, you can specify static IP addresses.

Public Network

A public network configuration allows your VM to communicate with the external network. In this mode, the VM can potentially obtain an IP address from the host network's DHCP server, making it accessible from the host machine and other devices on the network.

To set up a public network, modify your Vagrantfile as follows:

```
1  Vagrant.configure("2") do |config|
2    config.vm.define "machine1" do |machine1|
3      machine1.vm.network "public_network"
4    end
5  end
```

Note that using a public network might require additional network bridge configuration on the host machine.

Forwarded Ports

Port forwarding is a technique used to allow external devices to access services on a VM, bridging communication between the host and guest via specified ports.

Here's how to forward ports in your Vagrantfile:

```
1  Vagrant.configure("2") do |config|
2    config.vm.define "machine1" do |machine1|
```

```
3      machine1.vm.network "forwarded_port", guest: 80, host: 8080
4    end
5  end
```

This configuration forwards requests sent to port 8080 on the host machine to port 80 on the guest VM, which is useful for web development.

Networking Best Practices

When configuring networking for multiple VMs, consider the following best practices:

- Use private networks for inter-VM communication to enhance security.

- Utilize public networks sparingly and with a clear understanding of the security implications.

- Employ port forwarding for accessing specific services on VMs from the host machine, especially during development and testing phases.

Efficient use of networking in a multi-machine Vagrant environment allows for the simulation of more complex, scalable, and interconnected applications, closely mimicking production setups. Understanding and effectively leveraging these networking capabilities are crucial for software development and testing in a controlled and isolated manner.

5.4   Provisioning in a Multi-Machine Setup

Provisioning in a multi-machine setup with Vagrant involves automating the setup of software and configurations across all machines defined in a `Vagrantfile`. The primary goal of provisioning is to ensure each virtual machine (VM) is prepared with the necessary tools, software, and settings for the development environment to operate as intended. This not only saves time but also guarantees consistency across all VMs in the multi-machine environment.

For a comprehensive understanding, let's analyze how provisioning works in Vagrant, focusing on script-based and configuration management tool-based approaches.

Script-Based Provisioning

In the context of Vagrant, script-based provisioning is typically handled by shell scripts. These scripts are executed on the VM after it is booted and before it is made available for use. To provision multiple machines within the same Vagrantfile, each defined VM can have its own provisioning script.

The following is an example of defining multiple VMs in a Vagrantfile with specific provisioning scripts for each:

```
1   Vagrant.configure("2") do |config|
2     config.vm.define "web" do |web|
3       web.vm.box = "ubuntu/bionic64"
4       web.vm.provision "shell", path: "provision-web.sh"
5     end
6
7     config.vm.define "db" do |db|
8       db.vm.box = "ubuntu/bionic64"
9       db.vm.provision "shell", path: "provision-db.sh"
10    end
11  end
```

In this example, two VMs are defined: one for a web server and another for a database server. Each VM is provisioned using a different shell script, provision-web.sh for the web server and provision-db.sh for the database server. These scripts contain all necessary commands to install software, apply settings, and configure services on the VMs.

Configuration Management Tools

Besides script-based provisioning, Vagrant supports various configuration management tools such as Ansible, Chef, Puppet, and Salt.

These tools offer a higher level of abstraction, allowing for idempotent and repeatable configurations. Here is how to configure a multi-machine setup with an Ansible playbook:

```
1   Vagrant.configure("2") do |config|
2     config.vm.define "web" do |web|
3       web.vm.box = "ubuntu/bionic64"
4       web.vm.provision "ansible" do |ansible|
5         ansible.playbook = "playbook-web.yml"
6       end
7     end
8
9     config.vm.define "db" do |db|
10      db.vm.box = "ubuntu/bionic64"
11      db.vm.provision "ansible" do |ansible|
12        ansible.playbook = "playbook-db.yml"
13      end
14    end
15  end
```

In this configuration, two VMs are provisioned using Ansible playbooks. playbook-web.yml is dedicated to setting up the web server, whereas playbook-db.yml is used for the database server. Ansible playbooks allow for more sophisticated and readable configurations compared to shell scripts.

Provisioning Sequence

Understanding the provisioning sequence is crucial, especially in a multi-machine environment where dependencies might exist between machines. Vagrant executes the provisioning scripts or configuration management tool commands in the order they are defined for each VM. However, when parallel execution is enabled (Vagrant's default behavior when supported by the provider), the provisioning order across different VMs is not guaranteed.

To manage dependencies between machines, such as ensuring the database server is fully set up before the web server starts its provisioning process, Vagrant allows for the manual specification of the provisioning order:

```
1   config.vm.provision "shell", run: "always" do |s|
2     s.inline = "echo 'Provisioning order is essential'"
3   end
```

131

This provisioner is set to run "always", indicating it can be used to
check the state of other VMs or trigger provisioning sequences that
respect the required order of setup operations.

Provisioning in a multi-machine Vagrant setup provides a scalable
way to automate the configuration and management of VMs,
essential for developing complex, distributed applications.   By
leveraging script-based provisioning or advanced configuration
management tools, developers can establish a coherent and
repeatable environment across all VMs, streamlining the
development and testing processes.

5.5   Synchronizing Folders Across Multiple Machines

Synchronizing folders across multiple virtual machines (VMs)
within a Vagrant multi-machine environment is a critical task for
ensuring that files and directories maintain consistency across all
nodes involved in the development or testing process.   This is
especially relevant when sharing code bases, configuration files, or
data sets that must remain up-to-date on each VM to preserve the
integrity and functionality of the system being developed or tested.

To achieve folder synchronization in Vagrant, a shared folder mechanism is employed, which can be configured in the Vagrantfile. This
shared folder is accessible from all VMs defined in the environment,
allowing for real-time sharing and updating of files across machines.

Configuring Shared Folders

The configuration of shared folders is done in the Vagrantfile. Each
VM can be configured to share one or multiple folders with all other
VMs within the multi-machine setup. The basic syntax for configur-
ing a shared folder is as follows:

```
config.vm.synced_folder "host_folder/", "/vm_folder"
```

In this configuration, `"host_folder/"` represents the path to the folder on the host machine that you wish to share, and `"/vm_folder"` represents the path within the VM where the shared folder will be accessible. It is important to note that these paths must be absolute.

Example Configuration

Consider a scenario where two VMs, named web and db, need access to a shared folder containing configuration files. The following snippet demonstrates how to configure this shared folder within the Vagrantfile:

```
1  Vagrant.configure("2") do |config|
2    config.vm.define "web" do |web|
3      web.vm.synced_folder "./config/", "/var/shared/config"
4    end
5
6    config.vm.define "db" do |db|
7      db.vm.synced_folder "./config/", "/var/shared/config"
8    end
```

In this example, the `"./config/"` directory on the host is synchronized with the `"/var/shared/config"` directory on both the web and db VMs.

Synchronization Modes

Vagrant supports multiple synchronization modes, each with its own set of advantages and disadvantages. The default mode is VirtualBox shared folders, but other modes such as NFS, RSync, and SMB are also available. The choice of synchronization mode can impact the performance and reliability of file sharing across VMs, so it is crucial to select the mode that best suits the needs of your project.

VirtualBox Shared Folders

This is the default synchronization mode for Vagrant environments running on VirtualBox. It offers a balance between ease of use and performance but may not always provide the best file I/O performance.

NFS

Network File System (NFS) is a network-based file sharing protocol that can offer improved performance over VirtualBox shared folders, especially for projects with heavy file I/O requirements. However, it requires additional configuration and might not be supported on all operating systems out of the box.

RSync

RSync provides a one-way synchronization mechanism from the host to the guest VM. It is highly efficient for initial synchronization but requires manual intervention or additional automation to keep files up-to-date after the initial sync.

SMB

Server Message Block (SMB) is a synchronization mode mainly used in Windows environments. It offers good performance and ease of use but requires additional setup on non-Windows host machines.

Synchronizing folders across multiple machines in Vagrant is essential for seamless development and testing workflows. By leveraging Vagrant's shared folder feature and selecting the appropriate synchronization mode, teams can ensure that all VMs within a multi-machine environment have access to the necessary files and directories in real time.

5.6 Managing Dependencies Between Machines

Managing dependencies between machines in a multi-machine Vagrant environment is critical to ensure that the network of virtual machines (VMs) operates harmoniously. This encompasses coordinating the boot order, defining clear dependency chains, and automating the management process to the largest extent possible to reduce manual intervention and potential human errors.

Defining Dependency Chains

The first step in managing dependencies is defining the dependency chains explicitly. This specifies which machines are dependent on others for their configuration or operation. For instance, a web application server might depend on a database server being fully operational before it can start.

Utilizing Vagrant's native configuration files, you can define these chains by controlling the order of machine definitions and employing provisioning scripts that wait for dependencies to be satisfied before continuing. The following is an example where we specify a dependency of a web server on a database server:

```
Vagrant.configure("2") do |config|
  config.vm.define "db" do |db|
    db.vm.box = "mysql/server"
    # Configuration for the database server
  end

  config.vm.define "web" do |web|
    web.vm.box = "apache/server"
    # Ensure the database server is up and running
    web.vm.provision "shell", inline: <<-SHELL
      until nc -z db 3306; do
        echo "Waiting for database..."
        sleep 1
      done
    SHELL
    # Configuration for the web server
  end
```

135

In the above example, the web server uses a shell provisioner script that waits (using nc command for network connectivity checking) for the database server to be accessible on port 3306 before proceeding with its own setup.

Automating Dependency Management

Automating the startup and provisioning process based on these dependencies is vital to streamline operations. *Vagrant's triggers plugin* can be used to execute specific actions before or after commands like vagrant up, vagrant halt, etc., allowing for automation based on the defined dependencies.

Here's an example of using triggers to ensure that the database VM is started before the web server VM:

```
1  config.trigger.before :up, :vm => "web" do |trigger|
2    trigger.info = "Ensuring the database VM is running before starting the web VM.
        "
3    trigger.run = {inline: "vagrant up db"}
4  end
```

This ensures that the db VM is started before the web VM whenever the vagrant up web command is issued, reinforcing the dependency chain without manual oversight.

Best Practices

When managing dependencies between VMs, adhering to best practices can significantly reduce complexity and potential issues:

- Clearly document the dependencies and their order in the Vagrantfile or accompanying documentation to aid understanding and maintenance.

- Use provisioning scripts judiciously to automate the wait for dependency resolution wherever necessary.

- Employ Vagrant's plugin ecosystem, like the triggers plugin, to automate and enforce the dependency management process.

- Regularly test recovery from partial and complete outages to ensure dependency chains are accurately defined and that automation scripts handle restarts appropriately.

Managing dependencies between machines in a multi-machine environment with Vagrant requires careful planning, clear definition of dependencies, and automation to enforce and respect these dependencies. By doing so, you can create a robust, interconnected network of VMs that can automatically adapt to internal dependencies, thereby minimizing manual intervention and increasing development efficiency.

5.7 Allocating Resources in Multi-Machine Environments

Allocating resources in multi-machine environments is a pivotal task to ensure that each virtual machine (VM) operates efficiently without overstepping its bounds and affecting the performance of other VMs in the environment. Proper resource allocation avoids bottlenecks, ensuring that all services running across multiple machines do not experience performance degradation due to insufficient computing resources (CPU, memory, and disk I/O).

To begin with resource allocation, it is essential to understand that each VM defined within a Vagrantfile can have individual resource settings. These settings include but are not limited to the number of CPUs, the amount of memory, and the size of the disk. Vagrant interfaces with the underlying provider, such as VirtualBox, VMware, Hyper-V, or others, to configure these resources for each VM upon their initialization.

Configuring CPU and Memory

The allocation of CPU and memory resources to each VM can significantly impact the performance of the applications running inside them. The syntax for specifying CPU and memory allocation in a Vagrantfile is shown below:

```
1  config.vm.define "web" do |web|
2    web.vm.provider "virtualbox" do |v|
3      v.customize ["modifyvm", :id, "--cpus", "2"]
4      v.customize ["modifyvm", :id, "--memory", "2048"]
5    end
6  end
```

In the example above, a VM named web is configured with 2 CPUs and 2 GB of memory. These settings tell VirtualBox, the provider in this case, to allocate the specified resources to the VM. Adjusting these values allows developers to balance the resources based on the VM's workload.

Managing Disk I/O

Disk Input/Output (I/O) is another critical resource, especially for applications that perform numerous read and write operations to the disk. Controlling Disk I/O can help in minimizing the I/O wait times which, in turn, improves the overall application performance. Vagrant itself does not directly offer settings to adjust disk I/O; however, this can be achieved by interfacing with the provider's own tools or by adopting certain best practices, such as using solid-state drives (SSDs) for storage or distributing I/O-intensive applications across multiple disks.

Network Bandwidth

Network bandwidth is a resource often overlooked in multi-machine setups. Nevertheless, applications communicating over a network can be severely impacted by limited bandwidth. To manage network bandwidth, traffic shaping techniques or network simulation tools can be used. For instance, developers can use software like Wonder-Shaper or Trickle on Linux VMs to limit the bandwidth available to a VM, simulating more realistic network conditions.

Best Practices

- Always start with the minimum necessary resources for each VM and increase based on the actual demand observed during testing phases.

- Regularly monitor the performance and resource usage of VMs to adjust their allocations proactively.

- Use Vagrant's ability to provision machines with scripts to dynamically adjust resources based on workload requirements if supported by the provider.

- Consider the use of Vagrant plugins that enhance resource management capabilities, such as vagrant-cachier or vagrant-auto_network.

Careful planning and ongoing management of resources in multi-machine environments are essential for maintaining optimal performance and stability. Through the strategic allocation of CPU, memory, disk I/O, and network bandwidth, developers can ensure that their multi-VM setups are both efficient and reliable, thus facilitating smoother development and testing workflows.

5.8   Using Vagrant with Docker Containers

In this section, we will discuss the integration of Vagrant with Docker containers. This combination offers powerful capabilities, enabling developers to manage Docker environments with the same ease and flexibility as virtual machines through Vagrant.

First, it is essential to understand how Vagrant can control Docker containers. To facilitate this, Vagrant offers a Docker provider. Unlike traditional providers which manage virtual machines, the Docker provider allows Vagrant to manage Docker containers directly. This feature enables developers to use Docker as a backend for Vagrant environments, leveraging Docker's lightweight containerization technology.

To begin using Docker containers with Vagrant, one must first ensure that Docker is installed on the host system. Vagrant interacts with Docker installed on the host or through a Vagrant-managed virtual machine configured to run Docker. The choice between these options depends on the user's setup and personal preference.

The basic workflow for integrating Docker with Vagrant involves the following steps:

- Define a `Vagrantfile` that specifies Docker as the provider.

- Configure Docker-specific options within the `Vagrantfile`.

- Use standard Vagrant commands to manage the Docker containers.

An example `Vagrantfile` configuration that specifies Docker as the provider is shown below:

```
1  Vagrant.configure("2") do |config|
2    config.vm.provider "docker" do |d, override|
3      d.image = "hashicorp/precise64"
4      d.has_ssh = true
5    end
6  end
```

In this example, the Docker provider is configured to use the "hashicorp/precise64" Docker image. The `d.has_ssh = true` option is specified to enable SSH access to the container, similar to how one would access a virtual machine managed by Vagrant.

Next, let's discuss networking with Docker containers managed by Vagrant. Networking can be configured in the `Vagrantfile` to allow communication between the container and the host system, as well as between multiple containers managed by Vagrant. The configuration options include port forwarding, private networks, and public networks, mirroring the networking capabilities available for Vagrant-managed virtual machines.

For provisioning Docker containers managed by Vagrant, it is possible to use shell scripts, Ansible playbooks, Puppet manifests, or Chef cookbooks. This flexibility in provisioning methods allows developers to reuse existing scripts and automation tools with Docker containers, streamlining the setup of development and test environments.

Synchronizing folders between the host system and Docker containers is another key feature. By configuring shared folders in the Vagrantfile, developers can easily share source code and other resources between the host and containers, facilitating a seamless development workflow.

Using Vagrant with Docker containers provides a robust solution for managing containerized environments with ease. It combines Docker's efficient containerization with Vagrant's flexibility and ease of use, enabling developers to streamline their development, testing, and deployment workflows.

5.9   Scenario: Setting Up a Development and Testing Environment

Creating a cohesive environment for both development and testing is vital for the success of any project. In this scenario, we will illustrate the practical steps to configure a Vagrant environment that neatly splits between a development server and a testing server. This setup ensures that developers can work on features independently without affecting ongoing testing routines.

First, it is important to understand that each virtual machine (VM) in this setup will represent a distinct environment. We will use a single Vagrantfile to define both VMs, leveraging Vagrant's multi-machine functionality.

```
1   Vagrant.configure("2") do |config|
2
3      config.vm.define "dev" do |dev|
4         dev.vm.box = "ubuntu/bionic64"
5         dev.vm.network "private_network", type: "dhcp"
6         dev.vm.hostname = "development-server"
7         dev.vm.provision "shell", path: "setup_dev.sh"
8      end
9
10     config.vm.define "test" do |test|
```

141

```
11          test.vm.box = "ubuntu/bionic64"
12          test.vm.network "private_network", type: "dhcp"
13          test.vm.hostname = "testing-server"
14          test.vm.provision "shell", path: "setup_test.sh"
15      end
16
17  end
```

The above Vagrantfile instructs Vagrant to create two VMs, both based on Ubuntu 18.04 LTS (Bionic Beaver). Each machine has its distinct role, indicated by its name - "dev" for development and "test" for testing. They are configured to be on the same private network, allowing them to communicate directly if needed.

For provisioning, we have specified different shell scripts for each VM. The setup_dev.sh script should contain commands to install development tools, libraries, and any other software required for developing the application. Conversely, setup_test.sh would focus on the tools and configurations necessary for testing, such as test runners, databases in their specific test configurations, and any mock services.

With a configured environment, the next steps involve managing the interplay between these environments:

- Synchronizing code between the two machines is crucial. We recommend using a shared folder to allow changes made in the development environment to be immediately accessible in the testing environment.

- For complex projects, it might be necessary to introduce a continuous integration/continuous deployment (CI/CD) pipeline, which could automate the movement of code from development to testing and vice versa.

- Regularly updating the provisioning scripts to ensure that both environments stay aligned with the project's evolving dependencies and requirements.

Networking between the two VMs ensures that services running in the development environment can be accessed from the testing environment for integration tests. This setup models the interaction between components in a more production-like scenario, providing valuable insights into how the application behaves in a distributed environment.

Allocating sufficient resources to each VM is also critical, as the development environment might require more resources for IDEs and other development tools, while the testing environment might need additional memory or CPU for running intensive test suites. This can be configured by adding resource specifications within each block in the Vagrantfile, such as:

```
1   dev.vm.provider "virtualbox" do |vb|
2       vb.memory = "2048"
3       vb.cpus = 2
4   end
5
6   test.vm.provider "virtualbox" do |vb|
7       vb.memory = "4096"
8       vb.cpus = 4
9   end
```

In summary, configuring a development and testing environment with Vagrant involves defining multiple VMs within a single Vagrantfile, provisioning them according to their roles, and ensuring they can network with each other. This approach not only facilitates a seamless development workflow but also mirrors a realistic scenario where development and testing operate in tandem yet in isolated environments. Through meticulous setup and management, the development-testing divide can be efficiently bridged, significantly bolstering the software development lifecycle.

5.10   Scenario: Configuring a Web Server and Database Server

Configuring a multi-machine environment with Vagrant that comprises a web server and a database server is a pivotal skill for simulating production environments. This setup is instrumental for developers to test their applications in conditions that closely

143

mirror the live deployment scenario. The process involves defining both servers within a single Vagrantfile, establishing a private network for them to communicate, and provisioning each machine with the necessary software.

Let's begin with the definition of both virtual machines (VMs) in the Vagrantfile. It is imperative to assign unique names to each VM to differentiate their roles within our multi-machine setup.

```
1   Vagrant.configure("2") do |config|
2
3     config.vm.define "web" do |web|
4       web.vm.box = "ubuntu/bionic64"
5       web.vm.network "private_network", type: "dhcp"
6       web.vm.provision "shell", inline: <<-SHELL
7         apt update
8         apt install -y nginx
9       SHELL
10    end
11
12    config.vm.define "db" do |db|
13      db.vm.box = "ubuntu/bionic64"
14      db.vm.network "private_network", type: "dhcp"
15      db.vm.provision "shell", inline: <<-SHELL
16        apt update
17        apt install -y mysql-server
18      SHELL
19    end
20
21  end
```

In the preceding Vagrantfile excerpt, two VMs are defined: "web" for the web server and "db" for the database server. Both VMs are based on the "ubuntu/bionic64" box, which provides a stable and widely-compatible Ubuntu environment. The `private_network` option is configured with DHCP to allow the VMs to communicate with each other over a private network. The `provision` section includes shell scripts for installing Nginx on the web server and MySQL on the database server, highlighting the automation capabilities of Vagrant provisioning.

After defining the machines, the next step focuses on the networking aspect. The private network facilitates direct communication between the web and database servers without exposing them to the outside world. This setup mirrors production environments where web and database servers interact closely yet remain shielded from external access.

Executing vagrant up will bring both VMs online, applying the configurations and provisions specified.   Upon successful completion, the web server will be able to communicate with the database server over the private network. To validate this, one could SSH into the web server using vagrant ssh web and ping the database server using its private IP address, which should have been automatically assigned by DHCP.

```
ping <db-private-ip>
```

Output from this command should confirm the connectivity between the two servers. This step is crucial for troubleshooting any network configuration issues before proceeding with further application setup.

In terms of resource management, while the default settings in Vagrant are satisfactory for demonstration purposes, production-like environments necessitate tweaking. Adjusting CPU and memory allocation according to the demand of the services running on both the web and database servers ensures optimal performance. Vagrant allows this fine-tuning directly within the Vagrantfile:

```
1  web.vm.provider "virtualbox" do |v|
2    v.memory = 1024
3    v.cpus = 2
4  end
5
6  db.vm.provider "virtualbox" do |v|
7    v.memory = 2048
8    v.cpus = 2
9  end
```

The above code assigns 1GB of RAM and 2 CPUs to the web server, and 2GB of RAM and 2 CPUs to the database server. Adjusting these values is contingent upon the actual load anticipated on each server.

To summarize, setting up a multi-machine environment with a web server and database server using Vagrant involves defining VMs in a Vagrantfile, establishing a private network, provisioning with necessary software, and fine-tuning resources. This approach not only fosters a deeper understanding of how different components of a web application interact but also empowers developers to create and manage complex environments with ease.

5.11 Best Practices for Managing Multi-Machine Environments

Managing multi-machine environments efficiently entails adopting certain practices that ensure smooth deployment, operational efficiency, and easier maintenance. This section underscores the best practices pivotal for mastering multi-machine setups in Vagrant, guiding you through principles that not only streamline development workflows but also bolster your projects' resilience and scalability.

Optimizing Vagrantfile Configuration

The cornerstone of managing multi-machine environments effectively lies in the meticulous scripting of the 'Vagrantfile'. It defines configurations for each virtual machine (VM) and sets the stage for their interaction. Key practices include:

- **Using Loops for Similar Configurations:** When configuring multiple VMs that share common settings, utilize loops to avoid repetitive code blocks, enhancing readability and maintainability.

- **Parameterization:** Leverage variables for configurations that might vary between environments (e.g., VM memory allocation, CPU count). This approach aids in customizing environments without altering the core 'Vagrantfile' structure.

- **Comments:** Comprehensive commenting within your 'Vagrantfile' elucidates the purpose and functionality of code blocks, aiding in collective development efforts and future modifications.

146

Networking Strategies

Effective networking configuration between VMs is fundamental in simulating real-world deployment scenarios. Consider the following:

- **Private Networks for Inter-VM Communication:** Define private networks for communication between VMs, facilitating a controlled environment that mimics production network setups without exposing services to the external network unnecessarily.

- **Consistent IP Addressing:** Allocate static IP addresses to each VM, ensuring consistent access configurations and simplifying network management.

Provisioning Automation

Leverage automation tools for provisioning to streamline the setup process of your VMs:

- **Use Configuration Management Tools:** Employ tools like Ansible, Puppet, or Chef for automated provisioning. These tools ensure that all VMs are configured consistently, adhering to predefined specifications.

- **Scripting:** Incorporate shell scripts for initial provisioning tasks not covered by configuration management tools, ensuring full automation of the environment setup.

Resource Allocation

Appropriately allocating resources to each VM ensures optimal performance without overcommitting the host machine's capabilities:

- **Memory and CPU:** Assign memory and CPU resources based on the intended workload of each VM, ensuring balanced resource distribution that prevents bottlenecks.

- **Dynamic Scaling:** Utilize Vagrant plugins that allow for dynamic resource scaling based on workload, offering a balance between performance and resource utilization.

Continuous Monitoring and Logging

Implement monitoring and logging solutions across your multi-machine environment:

- **Monitoring Tools:** Use tools to monitor VM resource usage and application performance, facilitating early detection of issues that could impact development.

- **Centralized Logging:** Implement centralized logging for all VMs, simplifying troubleshooting and performance analysis by aggregating logs in a single accessible location.

Regular Backups and Version Control

Protect your environment against data loss and facilitate easy rollback in case of errors:

- **Backup Strategies:** Create regular backups of VM states and critical data, employing automated tools where possible to ensure consistency.

- **Version Control:** Use version control systems for your 'Vagrantfile' and provisioning scripts, enabling you to track changes and revert to previous configurations if necessary.

Adhering to these best practices not only enhances the manageability of multi-machine environments but also contributes to the stability and efficiency of development workflows. By embedding these principles within your development process, you can exploit the full potential of Vagrant in creating complex, yet manageable, virtualized environments that closely replicate your production setups.

5.12 Common Pitfalls and How to Avoid Them

In multi-machine environments constructed with Vagrant, several common pitfalls can significantly impede the development process if not properly addressed. This section delineates these pitfalls and prescribes methodologies to circumvent them.

Inadequate Resource Allocation

One frequently encountered issue is the inadequate allocation of resources to virtual machines (VMs), leading to performance degradation or system instability. To mitigate this, it is imperative to:

- Estimate the resource usage of your applications on each VM and allocate resources accordingly.

- Regularly monitor VM performance and adjust allocations as necessary using Vagrant's configuration options.

For example, to modify the CPU and memory allocation in a Vagrantfile, you could use:

```
1  config.vm.provider "virtualbox" do |vb|
2    vb.memory = "2048"
3    vb.cpus = 2
4  end
```

Networking Conflicts

Configuring networking in a multi-machine environment can lead to conflicts, especially when similar configurations are applied without customization. To avoid such conflicts:

- Ensure each VM has a unique private network IP.

- Utilize different ports for services running on different VMs to avoid collision.

Network configuration example:

```
1  config.vm.define "web" do |web|
2    web.vm.network "private_network", ip: "192.168.50.4"
3  end
4
5  config.vm.define "db" do |db|
6    db.vm.network "private_network", ip: "192.168.50.5"
7  end
```

Provisioning Errors

Provisioning scripts can fail for various reasons, such as missing dependencies or incorrect script paths. Preventing these errors can be assisted by:

- Testing provisioning scripts independently before incorporating them into the Vagrant environment.

- Keeping provisioning scripts version-controlled and up to date.

Version Incompatibilities

Working with a multi-machine setup can introduce version incompatibilities among the Vagrant software, the provider (e.g., VirtualBox, VMware), and the box images used. To avoid these issues:

- Regularly update Vagrant, providers, and box images, while ensuring they are compatible.

- Specify exact versions of box images in the Vagrantfile to guarantee consistency across different development setups.

Example of specifying a box version:

```
1  config.vm.box = "ubuntu/xenial64"
2  config.vm.box_version = "20190514.0.0"
```

Synchronization Issues

Synchronizing files and folders across multiple VMs can lead to inconsistencies if not properly managed. To prevent synchronization issues:

- Utilize Vagrant's built-in synchronization mechanisms or third-party tools specifically designed for this purpose.

- Ensure consistent folder structures and paths across VMs.

By proactively addressing these common pitfalls, developers can significantly improve the robustness and efficiency of multi-machine environments managed with Vagrant. Adopting best practices not only facilitates smoother development workflows but also enhances the overall reliability of the virtual infrastructure.

Chapter 6

Managing State with Snapshots

Managing State with Snapshots is a powerful feature in Vagrant that allows users to save the current state of a virtual machine and revert back to that state at any time. Snapshots are invaluable for testing changes without the risk of permanently affecting the virtual machine, enabling developers to experiment freely and safely. By utilizing snapshots, teams can streamline the development process, quickly rollback to a stable state after testing new features or updates, and ensure consistency across different stages of development. This chapter will discuss how to effectively use snapshots within Vagrant, including creating, managing, and restoring them, as well as best practices for integrating snapshot management into your development workflow.

6.1   Understanding Snapshots in Virtualized Environments

Snapshots function as a powerful mechanism within virtualized environments, enabling users to capture the exact state of a virtual machine (VM) at any given moment. This capability is akin to taking a comprehensive photograph of the VM's current condition, encompassing its operating system, software applications, and all data files. When a snapshot is created, it preserves the state and data of a VM at a specific point in time. This preserved state can include everything from the VM's system settings and installed software to the current data in memory and on disk.

To grasp the technical underpinnings of snapshots, it is essential to understand how they interact with the virtual environment's storage system. When a snapshot is taken, the virtualization platform momentarily halts all write operations to the VM's disk. Instead of altering the original disk files, any subsequent changes are written to a new differential disk. This differential disk, often referred to as a "delta" disk, records only the changes made since the snapshot was created. As a result, the original disk remains unaltered, preserving the VM's state at the moment the snapshot was taken.

The mechanism of a snapshot can be better understood with the help of the following lstlisting illustrating a simplified command to create a snapshot in Vagrant:

```
1   vagrant snapshot save my_first_snapshot
```

The command above instructs Vagrant to create a snapshot of the current state of the virtual machine and assigns it the name my_first_snapshot. This snapshot captures the complete state of the VM, including its disk data, memory content, and device configurations.

Snapshots can be nested, creating a hierarchy or a chain of snapshots. This structure allows users to revert the VM back to any previous state captured by a snapshot, not just the most recent one. For example, if a series of snapshots were taken at different stages of a VM's configuration, users could choose to revert the VM to any one of these saved states.

Taking snapshots incurs minimal immediate overhead but can lead to increased storage requirements. This is because each differential disk associated with a snapshot must store the information necessary to recreate the changes made since the previous snapshot. As more snapshots are taken, more differential disks are created, potentially leading to significant usage of storage space over time.

Snapshots offer a multitude of benefits for managing virtual environments efficiently. They facilitate experimentation by allowing changes to be made and tested without the risk of permanently altering the VM's stable state. If changes result in undesirable outcomes, users can effortlessly revert to a prior state using the snapshot feature. Consequently, snapshots become an integral tool for developers and IT professionals in testing applications, updates, and system configurations within a controlled and reversible framework.

However, effective management of snapshots is crucial to avoiding "snapshot sprawl" - a condition where numerous outdated or unnecessary snapshots consume excessive storage resources. Prudent snapshot management practices involve regularly reviewing and deleting unneeded snapshots and understanding the impact of snapshot operations on overall system performance.

Snapshots in virtualized environments offer a robust method for safeguarding VM states, enabling safe experimentation and efficient rollback capabilities. By understanding the underlying mechanics and employing snapshots judiciously within their workflows, developers and IT professionals can leverage the full potential of this feature to enhance their development and operational efficiencies.

6.2   The Benefits of Using Snapshots with Vagrant

Snapshots provide a robust mechanism for preserving the exact state of a virtual machine (VM) at a specific point in time. This capability becomes indispensable in a variety of scenarios encountered during software development and testing. The integration of snapshots within Vagrant offers several advantages, making it a critical tool for developers aiming to enhance their development environments.

- **Facilitates Experimentation**: One of the primary benefits of using snapshots with Vagrant is the freedom it offers to developers for experimentation. Running tests on new software versions, configurations, or exploring new development approaches without the concern of irrevocably altering the development environment is made possible. If the changes prove unsuccessful or lead to unexpected results, reverting to a saved snapshot restores the VM to its previous state.

- **Speeds Up Development Process**: The ability to quickly revert a VM to a previously saved state accelerates the development process. Instead of spending time troubleshooting or reconfiguring the VM to its initial state, developers can simply roll back to a snapshot, saving valuable time and effort.

- **Enhances Collaboration**: Snapshots contribute to a more seamless collaboration among team members. Teams can share specific VM states by distributing the corresponding snapshots. This ensures that all team members are working in identical development environments, reducing discrepancies and incompatibilities.

- **Simplifies Complex Testing Scenarios**: Snapshots are particularly useful in testing complex scenarios that require the VM to be in a specific state. For example, testing database migrations, software updates, or backward compatibility of new software releases can be easily managed by reverting to the appropriate snapshots as needed.

- **Acts as a Safety Net**: Snapshots act as a safety net, allowing developers to return to a known stable state in the event of a failure. This reduces the risk associated with trying out new software or making significant changes to the VM.

- **Optimizes Resource Utilization**: By leveraging snapshots, developers can maintain multiple states of a single VM without the need for duplicating the VM entirely. This efficient use of resources is particularly beneficial in environments with limited computing resources.

To illustrate the process of creating a snapshot in Vagrant, consider the following command:

```
1  $ vagrant snapshot save my_snapshot
```

This command will create a snapshot of the current state of the VM and name it my_snapshot. Snapshots are uniquely identified by their names, allowing for easy management and restoration.

The integration of snapshots with Vagrant significantly enhances the development and testing workflows by providing flexibility, increasing efficiency, and offering a failsafe mechanism. The advantages of using snapshots extend beyond individual convenience, facilitating better team collaboration and contributing to a more robust and error-tolerant development process.

6.3 Creating Snapshots: Basics and Commands

Creating snapshots in Vagrant is a straightforward process that involves using several key commands within the Vagrant environment. These commands allow users to save the current state of a virtual machine, essentially capturing a 'picture' of the VM at a specific point in time. This is invaluable for development, testing, and version control purposes, offering a quick way to revert to a known good state whenever needed.

The primary command for creating snapshots is `vagrant snapshot save`. This command requires at least one argument: the name you wish to assign to the snapshot. This name is important as it serves as an identifier for the snapshot, allowing for easy reference when you want to restore or manage this saved state later. Here's how the command is structured:

```
1   vagrant snapshot save [vm-name] snapshot-name
```

If you're working with a multi-machine environment, you can specify the VM name before the snapshot name. Otherwise, Vagrant will default to the primary machine in a single VM setup. It's crucial to select meaningful, descriptive names for each snapshot to ensure they can be easily identified and managed.

Upon executing this command, Vagrant will initiate the process of saving the current state of the specified VM. This includes all aspects of the VM, such as its file system, currently installed software, configuration settings, and even the state of network interfaces. Here is an example of creating a snapshot named `pre-update`:

```
1   vagrant snapshot save pre-update
```

The output will resemble the following, indicating that the snapshot process has been successfully initiated and completed:

```
==> default: Snapshotting the machine as 'pre-update'...
==> default: Snapshot saved! You can restore the snapshot at any time by
using `vagrant snapshot restore`. You can delete it using
`vagrant snapshot delete`.
```

After creating snapshots, managing them becomes equally important. To list all snapshots for a given VM, the following command is used:

```
1   vagrant snapshot list [vm-name]
```

This command outputs a list of all snapshots taken for the VM, providing a quick overview of the available restore points. It's a good practice to regularly review this list and manage snapshots effectively, ensuring that only necessary snapshots are kept, thus optimizing storage and performance.

Creating and managing snapshots with Vagrant are fundamental tasks for maintaining flexible, robust, and revertible development environments. By incorporating these practices into your workflow, you can significantly reduce the risk associated with testing new features or making significant changes, secure in the knowledge that you can easily revert to a previous state if needed.

6.4   Managing Snapshots: Listing, Restoring, and Removing

Managing snapshots effectively is a crucial aspect of ensuring a smooth and efficient development process. This section will cover the essential commands and practices for listing, restoring, and removing snapshots in Vagrant environments.

Listing Snapshots

To gain an overview of the snapshots associated with a Vagrant environment, the 'vagrant snapshot list' command is used. This command provides a comprehensive list of all snapshots taken, denoted by their names.

```
1    $ vagrant snapshot list
```

This command will output a list resembling the following:

```
default
    snapshot1
    snapshot2
```

Each entry under the Vagrant machine's name represents a snapshot in the order they were created.

Restoring Snapshots

Restoring a snapshot is as simple as reverting the state of your virtual machine to a previously captured snapshot. To restore a snapshot, one must use the 'vagrant snapshot restore' command followed by the name of the snapshot to be restored.

```
1   $ vagrant snapshot restore snapshot1
```

Upon execution, Vagrant will revert the virtual machine to the state it was in at the time of the snapshot. This action is particularly useful for returning to a stable state before testing new features or updates.

Removing Snapshots

Over time, the accumulation of snapshots can consume significant disk space. Consequently, it is advisable to remove unnecessary snapshots. To delete a snapshot, the 'vagrant snapshot delete' command is used, followed by the name of the snapshot to be removed.

```
1   $ vagrant snapshot delete snapshot2
```

This command will remove the specified snapshot from the list of available snapshots, freeing up disk space.

Best Practices

When managing snapshots, it is recommended to:

- Frequently list snapshots to keep track of the available states to which you can revert.

- Regularly restore snapshots during the development process to verify the stability and functionality of your code.

- Periodically remove old or unnecessary snapshots to conserve disk space and maintain an organized snapshot list.

Furthermore, naming snapshots in a clear, descriptive manner at the time of creation can significantly enhance the manageability of snapshots. For instance, naming a snapshot after a specific feature or testing phase can make it easier to identify the appropriate snapshot to restore when needed.

By following these practices and effectively utilizing the snapshot management commands, developers can leverage snapshots to facilitate a more efficient and error-resilient development workflow.

6.5 Snapshot Best Practices: When to Use and When Not to

Snapshots, while inherently powerful, require judicious use to maximize their benefits while minimizing potential drawbacks. This segment outlines the best practices for employing snapshots within your Vagrant environment, advising on appropriate and inadvisable contexts for their use.

When to Use Snapshots

The following scenarios highlight when it is advantageous to leverage snapshots:

- **Before Implementing Major Changes**: Prior to introducing significant modifications—whether they are configuration updates, software upgrades, or extensive code alterations—creating a snapshot can act as a safeguard. This practice ensures that, if the new changes introduce instability or undesired behavior, you can quickly revert to the pre-change state.

- **For Development and Testing Cycles**: Snapshots can profoundly streamline development and testing workflows. By snapshotting a stable development or test environment, developers can experiment without fear of irreversibly altering the base setup. This is particularly useful for testing the impact of different configurations or libraries on the application being developed.

- **To Facilitate Consistent Environments Across Teams**: When working in team environments, ensuring every member operates on a consistent and stable development platform is crucial. Snapshots can be used to capture such an environment, which can then be shared and restored across all team members' machines, fostering uniformity and predictability in development efforts.

- **When Learning New Technology**: For those venturing into unfamiliar technologies or architectures, snapshots provide a safety net. Learners can freely explore and manipulate the virtual environment with the assurance that they can easily undo mistakes or revert to a known good state by restoring a snapshot.

When Not to Use Snapshots

Conversely, there are circumstances where using snapshots may not be ideal:

- **As a Substitute for Version Control**: Snapshots should not replace version control systems (VCS) for managing code changes. While they can capture the state of a virtual machine at a point in time, snapshots are not designed for tracking incremental code changes or facilitating collaboration among developers. It's crucial to use appropriate VCS tools for code management, alongside snapshots for environment state management.

- **For Long-term Backup Purposes**: Relying on snapshots as a long-term backup solution is not advisable due to their performance impact and storage requirements. Snapshots can quickly grow in size, particularly if many changes are made to the disk after a snapshot is taken. For lasting backups of critical data or configurations, traditional backup solutions should be employed.

- **Without Regular Cleanup**: Left unmanaged, snapshots can accumulate, leading to degraded performance and excessive disk space consumption. It's essential to periodically review and remove outdated or unnecessary snapshots, retaining only those that serve an immediate or foreseeable purpose in the development lifecycle.

Automating Snapshot Management: To streamline the creation and cleanup of snapshots, consider the implementation of automation scripts or tools. Various Vagrant plugins and third-party utilities offer capabilities for scheduling snapshot creation and enforcing retention policies, helping to maintain an optimal balance between flexibility and resource utilization.

Snapshots are a robust tool in the developer's arsenal, offering a combination of safety, convenience, and efficiency. However, like all powerful tools, they require thoughtful application. Adhering to the best practices outlined above will ensure snapshots enhance your development workflow without introducing unnecessary complexity or overhead.

6.6 Using Snapshots for Development Workflows

Snapshots, as previously discussed, serve as a fundamental tool in preserving the state of a virtual machine (VM) at a specific point in time. In the context of development workflows, snapshots provide a versatile mechanism for developers to experiment, test, and rollback changes in a controlled and risk-free manner. This section delves into practical methodologies for embedding snapshot management within development operation cycles, thereby enhancing productivity and ensuring stability.

The integration of snapshots into development workflows can be segmented into various stages: preparation, development, testing, and maintenance. Each stage benefits from snapshots in unique ways, thus tailoring their usage to specific needs is crucial.

- **Preparation Stage**: Before diving into new features or updates, it is advisable to create a baseline snapshot. This snapshot acts as a reference point or 'clean state' from which to commence development. Executing the command within a Vagrant environment can achieve this:

```
1    vagrant snapshot save clean-state
```

  This command saves the current state of the VM as 'clean-state', which can later be restored if needed.

- **Development Stage**: During the development phase, developers may create multiple incremental snapshots to mark significant progress points. This practice enables developers to explore different implementation approaches without fear of irreversibly altering the system. For instance, after a new feature implementation, a snapshot can be taken:

```
1    vagrant snapshot save feature-x
```

- **Testing Stage**: Once development is complete, the application or feature undergoes testing. Should an issue arise, the ability to revert the VM to a pre-testing state quickly is invaluable. This is where snapshots shine, allowing for rapid testing cycles without the need for time-consuming environment reconfigurations. Restoring a snapshot is simple:

```
1    vagrant snapshot restore feature-x
```

  This command reverts the VM to the state when 'feature-x' snapshot was taken.

- **Maintenance Stage**: In maintaining a development environment, snapshots aid in the periodic cleanup and reversion to a known-good state. Before conducting significant updates or system-wide changes, taking a snapshot ensures a fallback option is readily available:

```
1    vagrant snapshot save pre-update
```

Beyond these stages, snapshots facilitate the exploration of different development paths, debugging, and sharing of stable VM states among team members, promoting consistency and collaboration. However, judicious use of snapshots is recommended to avoid performance degradation, as discussed in the previous section on performance considerations.

Automation plays a pivotal role in maximizing the effectiveness of snapshots within development workflows. Automating the creation and restoration of snapshots, as part of a continuous integration/continuous deployment (CI/CD) pipeline, can significantly reduce manual overhead and ensure consistent state management. Tools like Jenkins, GitLab CI, and others can be configured to perform snapshot operations in response to various triggers, such as pre-merge requests or after successful builds.

Moreover, integrating snapshot management with source control systems enables developers to link VM states to specific code commits or branches, thus further enhancing the traceability and reproducibility of development environments.

In summary, leveraging snapshots in development workflows offers a powerful means to safeguard progress, streamline testing and debugging processes, and ensure stability across development cycles. Careful planning and automation of snapshot operations can amplify these benefits, providing a robust framework for managing virtualized development environments.

6.7 Troubleshooting with Snapshots

Troubleshooting issues related to snapshots can often seem daunting, but with a systematic approach, many common problems can be resolved efficiently. This section outlines key troubleshooting strategies and solutions for frequent snapshot-related issues faced when using Vagrant.

Snapshot Does Not Reflect Current State

One common issue is finding that a snapshot does not accurately reflect the expected state of a virtual machine. This discrepancy usually occurs due to performing the snapshot operation while the virtual machine is in an inconsistent state or due to errors during the snapshot process.

```
1   # To ensure a consistent state, halt the virtual machine before taking a snapshot
2   vagrant halt
3   # Proceed to take a snapshot after the machine is halted
4   vagrant snapshot save snapshot_name
```

Always verify the virtual machine's state by accessing it directly or checking the logs to confirm that it is ready to be snapshot.

Snapshot Restoration Failure

Sometimes, attempts to restore a snapshot may fail, often leaving an error message indicating the nature of the problem. Common causes for restoration failures include corrupted snapshot files or conflicts with the current state of the virtual machine.

To address restoration failures, first, ensure the integrity of the snapshot file:

```
Error: Snapshot 'snapshot_name' could not be restored. The snapshot file is corrupted.
```

If the snapshot file is indeed corrupted and cannot be repaired, consider using an earlier snapshot if available. Additionally, reviewing Vagrant and VirtualBox (or alternative provider) logs can provide insights into the failure:

```
1   # Check Vagrant logs
2   cat .vagrant/machines/default/virtualbox/logs/vbox.log
3   # Inspect for any errors or warnings that might explain the restoration issue
```

Performance Degradation after Restoring Snapshots

Restoring snapshots can sometimes lead to performance degradation. This degradation typically results from discrepancies between the state of the virtual machine at the snapshot and the state of the development environment or dependencies when the snapshot is restored.

To mitigate this issue:

- Ensure that all dependencies are up to date after restoring a snapshot.

- Reboot the virtual machine after restoration to clear any transient states that may cause performance issues.

```
1   vagrant reload
```

- If the issue persists, consider taking a new snapshot of the updated state after troubleshooting to ensure smoother performance in future restorations.

Inability to Take Snapshots

In some cases, you may encounter difficulties when attempting to take snapshots. These difficulties could stem from insufficient disk space, permissions issues, or limitations imposed by the Vagrant provider in use.

To troubleshoot, first check available disk space:

```
1   df -h
```

If disk space is limited, free up space or adjust your environment to allocate more resources to the virtual machine. Additionally, verify that Vagrant and the virtualization provider (e.g., VirtualBox, VMware) have the necessary permissions to access and modify files related to snapshots.

Snapshot and Source Tree Mismatch

A mismatch between the snapshot state and the source tree can occur, especially if source code changes are made outside of the control
of Vagrant snapshots. This can lead to difficulties in matching the
virtual machine's state to the current development state.

To resolve this:

- Before taking a snapshot, ensure that all necessary changes are
  committed to source control. This practice enables easy
  reversion to the exact development state when a snapshot was
  taken.

- Use Vagrant's shared folders feature to maintain a consistent
  link between the host machine's source tree and the virtual machine, reducing discrepancies.

Troubleshooting snapshots requires a combination of preemptive
measures and reactive solutions. By following the outlined
strategies, developers can effectively manage snapshots, enhance
their development workflow, and ensure that their environment
remains consistent and reliable.

6.8   Automating   Snapshot   Creation   and Cleanup

Automating the process of creating and cleaning up snapshots is
crucial for maintaining a clean and manageable virtual
environment, especially when it comes to handling multiple virtual
machines or snapshots. This can be achieved through scripting and
scheduling these tasks, which not only saves valuable time but also
reduces the risk of human error.

Automating Snapshot Creation

To facilitate the automation of snapshot creation, one must understand the command-line utilities provided by Vagrant. The command to create a snapshot is `vagrant snapshot save`, followed by the name you wish to assign to the snapshot. Here is an example:

```
1  vagrant snapshot save [vm-name] snapshot-name
```

where [vm-name] is optional and specifies the target virtual machine by name, and snapshot-name is the name you want to give to the snapshot.

For automating this process, a simple shell script can be created. This script could be scheduled to run at regular intervals using cron jobs (for Unix-based systems) or Task Scheduler (for Windows). Here's an example script:

```
1  #!/bin/bash
2  # Snapshot name based on current date and time
3  SNAPSHOT_NAME=$(date +"%Y-%m-%d_%H-%M-%S")
4  vagrant snapshot save "my-vm" "$SNAPSHOT_NAME"
```

This script generates a unique snapshot name based on the current date and time, ensuring that snapshots are not overwritten and can be easily identified.

Automating Snapshot Cleanup

Over time, accumulating snapshots can consume significant disk space, thus necessitating their cleanup. Automating snapshot removal requires a careful but straightforward approach, ensuring that only older or specific snapshots are deleted, preserving recent and essential snapshots.

One method is to list all snapshots for a virtual machine, parse the output, and remove snapshots that meet certain criteria (e.g., older than a specific date). Here is an approach using Vagrant commands combined with shell scripting:

```
1  #!/bin/bash
2  # Define VM name and snapshot age limit
```

169

```
3   VM_NAME="my-vm"
4   AGE_LIMIT=30 # days
5
6   # List snapshots and filter those older than the specified AGE_LIMIT
7   vagrant snapshot list "$VM_NAME" | grep -Eo '^[0-9]{10}_[0-9]{8}' | while read
        SNAPSHOT_NAME; do
8     SNAPSHOT_DATE=$(echo $SNAPSHOT_NAME | cut -d"_" -f1)
9     # Convert snapshot date to seconds
10    SNAPSHOT_TIMESTAMP=$(date -d $SNAPSHOT_DATE +%s)
11    # Calculate the age limit in seconds
12    LIMIT_TIMESTAMP=$(($(date +%s) - AGE_LIMIT*24*60*60))
13    if [ $SNAPSHOT_TIMESTAMP -lt $LIMIT_TIMESTAMP ]; then
14      echo "Removing snapshot: $SNAPSHOT_NAME"
15      vagrant snapshot delete "$VM_NAME" "$SNAPSHOT_NAME"
16    else
17      echo "Retaining snapshot: $SNAPSHOT_NAME"
18    fi
19  done
```

This script first lists all snapshots for a specified VM, then filters those based on a naming convention that includes a datestamp. It compares the date of each snapshot against the defined age limit and deletes snapshots older than this limit.

Scheduling the Automation Tasks

As previously mentioned, snapshot creation and cleanup scripts can be scheduled to run at regular intervals. Utilizing crontab on Unix-based systems or Task Scheduler on Windows allows these tasks to run automatically without manual intervention. For example, to schedule the snapshot creation script to run daily at midnight on a Unix-based system, the following crontab entry could be used:

```
0 0 * * * /path/to/snapshot_creation_script.sh
```

For cleanup, you might schedule the script to run weekly:

```
0 0 * * 0 /path/to/snapshot_cleanup_script.sh
```

Integrating snapshot management into automated processes optimizes resources and enhances the efficiency and reliability of working with Vagrant environments. Through careful scheduling and scripting, developers can ensure their virtual environments remain functional, streamlined, and free from clutter.

6.9 Performance Considerations with Snapshots

When employing snapshots in a development environment, it is paramount to understand the implications they may have on system performance. This revolves around two primary axes: disk usage and speed of operations. Effectively managing these aspects is crucial to ensure that the benefits of snapshots do not inadvertently degrade the performance of the virtual machine or the host system.

Disk Usage

Each snapshot taken creates a new file that stores the current state of the virtual machine. These files are incremental, meaning a snapshot only contains the changes from the last state. Initially, this might seem efficient, but without proper management, snapshots can rapidly consume disk space. The following factors contribute to disk space usage:

- **Frequency of Snapshots:** More frequent snapshots lead to more incremental files, increasing disk space usage over time.

- **Magnitude of Changes:** If significant changes occur between snapshots (e.g., large file downloads or software installations), each snapshot can become substantially large.

- **Total Number of Snapshots:** Keeping a large number of snapshots adds up, consuming vast amounts of disk space.

To mitigate disk usage, regular maintenance of snapshots is advised. This includes deleting obsolete snapshots and consolidating changes when practical.

Speed of Operations

While snapshots provide the convenience of reverting to a known good state, they can impact the performance of virtual machines. The impact is particularly noticeable in the following areas:

- **Startup Time:** Starting a virtual machine with multiple snapshots can take longer, as the virtualization software needs to reconcile changes across all snapshots.

- **Operational Speed:** Virtual machines may run slower, especially when accessing files that have multiple different states across snapshots, as the system needs to navigate through the snapshot chain to retrieve the correct data.

To minimize performance degradation, it is recommended to maintain a judicious number of snapshots and restore to a baseline snapshot periodically, reducing the snapshot chain's length.

Balancing Snapshots and Performance

Finding the right balance between leveraging the utility of snapshots and maintaining optimal performance involves a few strategies:

- **Snapshot Scheduling:** Taking snapshots during times of low activity can mitigate performance impacts during peak operational hours.

- **Regular Cleanup:** As previously mentioned, routinely deleting old snapshots and consolidating changes can help manage disk space effectively and keep the virtual machine running smoothly.

- **Resource Allocation:** Allocating additional resources (e.g., disk space, RAM) to the host system or virtual machines can help compensate for performance overhead introduced by snapshots.

Finally, it is essential to monitor the performance and disk usage regularly to identify potential bottlenecks early and adjust the snapshot strategy accordingly. This proactive approach ensures that snapshots remain a valuable tool in the development process without compromising the system's efficiency.

6.10 Snapshots and Source Control Integration

Integrating snapshots with source control systems offers an advanced level of management and rollback for development environments. This integration enables teams to associate specific code commits with corresponding states of the development environment captured in snapshots. This section discusses the methodology, benefits, and considerations of combining these two powerful tools.

To begin, it is important to understand the significance of aligning the state of the development environment with the codebase. This alignment ensures that every member of the development team can replicate an environment that matches the historical code state, thus reducing "works on my machine" scenarios and fostering a more collaborative and consistent development process.

Methodology for Integration

The integration process typically involves the following steps:

- Whenever a significant change is made to the codebase and committed to the source control, a corresponding snapshot of the development environment is created. This snapshot should be uniquely identifiable, ideally tagged with the commit hash from the source control system.

- Information about the snapshot, such as its identifier (e.g., commit hash), snapshot name, and creation date, is then recorded in a file within the code repository. This ensures that the snapshot information is available to all team members and is version-controlled.

- To revert the development environment to the state corresponding to a specific code commit, a team member can look up the commit's associated snapshot identifier from the file, and use Vagrant commands to restore the snapshot.

Benefits

Integrating snapshots with source control yields several key benefits:

- **Environment Replicability:** Ensures that any team member can replicate the same development environment state associated with any code commit, enhancing consistency across the development team.

- **Enhanced Troubleshooting:** Facilitates easier identification and troubleshooting of issues introduced at specific points in the development history, by allowing developers to quickly revert to the exact state of the environment when the code was committed.

- **Efficient Collaboration:** Streamlines collaboration among team members working on different features or branches by allowing seamless switching between environment states aligned with different code bases.

Considerations

While integrating snapshots with source control brings many advantages, there are considerations to be mindful of:

- **Storage Space:** Snapshots, particularly multiple snapshots over time, can consume significant disk space. Efficient management and cleanup of snapshots are necessary to mitigate this.

- **Performance:** Depending on the virtualization technology and the size of the development environment, creating and restoring snapshots can have a performance impact. It is recommended to gauge this impact and adjust the snapshot strategy accordingly.

- **Automation:** Automating the snapshot creation and association with code commits requires scripting and configuration. This setup time needs to be considered in the overall integration strategy.

Through these methodologies, benefits, and considerations, integrating snapshots with source control systems emerges as a robust strategy for enhancing development workflows, facilitating greater consistency, and enabling efficient collaboration and troubleshooting within development teams.

6.11 Advanced Snapshot Management: Tools and Techniques

Advanced snapshot management extends beyond the basic 'vagrant snapshot' commands, offering ways to optimize, automate, and effectively integrate snapshots within a development workflow. This section explores tools and techniques designed to enhance the capabilities and efficiency of working with snapshots in Vagrant environments.

Automating Snapshot Creation with Triggers

Vagrant Triggers provide a powerful mechanism to automate the process of taking snapshots at specific instances or events within the Vagrant lifecycle. This automation ensures that snapshots are created consistently, without manual intervention, thereby reducing the risk of human error.

To implement an automated snapshot before halting a virtual machine, the following configuration can be added to the Vagrantfile:

```
config.trigger.before :halt do |trigger|
  trigger.name = "Creating snapshot before halting"
  trigger.run = {inline: "vagrant snapshot save before-halt"}
end
```

This trigger automatically saves a snapshot named 'before-halt' each time the 'vagrant halt' command is executed, ensuring that the current state is preserved before the machine is powered off.

Snapshot Management with Third-Party Tools

In addition to Vagrant's built-in snapshot capabilities, there are third-party tools which offer enhanced features for snapshot management. One such tool is 'Snaptree', which introduces the concept of snapshot trees, allowing developers to create, manage, and navigate between snapshots in a hierarchical structure.

With 'Snaptree', snapshots can be organized in a way that reflects the development workflow, making it easier to return to specific states or branches of development. Installation and usage instructions for these tools are generally available on their respective websites or repositories.

Integrating Snapshots into Continuous Integration/Continuous Deployment (CI/CD) Pipelines

Snapshots can be an integral part of CI/CD pipelines, particularly for testing and rollback purposes. By integrating snapshot creation and restoration into pipeline stages, it is possible to automate the testing of code in isolated environments, and gracefully rollback changes if tests fail.

One approach to integrating snapshots with CI/CD is by using scriptable interfaces provided by CI/CD tools (such as Jenkins,

GitLab CI, etc.) to issue Vagrant snapshot commands based on pipeline events. For instance, a pipeline job could be configured to:

- Create a snapshot of the virtual machine before deploying new changes.

- Run automated tests against the deployed changes.

- Restore the snapshot if tests fail, ensuring that the virtual machine is returned to its previous state.

Performance Considerations

While snapshots offer flexibility and safety, they also introduce overhead that can impact the performance of the virtual machine and consume additional disk space. It is important to strike a balance between the convenience of snapshots and the resources they consume. Techniques to mitigate performance degradation include:

- Regularly cleaning up unnecessary snapshots, especially those that are no longer relevant to the development workflow.

- Limiting the depth of snapshot trees to reduce complexity and storage requirements.

- Using differential snapshots, which only save changes made since the last snapshot, to minimize disk space usage.

Advanced snapshot management involves leveraging automation, third-party tools, and CI/CD integration to enhance the utility of snapshots in development workflows. By adopting these advanced techniques, teams can maximize the benefits of snapshots while minimizing their drawbacks.

6.12   Limitations and Caveats of Snapshots

Snapshots, while incredibly versatile in managing virtual machine states, come with their own set of limitations and potential pitfalls that users must navigate.   Understanding these constraints is essential for leveraging snapshots effectively without falling prey to common issues that might hinder the development workflow or, worse, lead to data loss.

Firstly, it is important to highlight that the use of snapshots increases storage requirements. Every snapshot taken is essentially a point-in-time image of the virtual machine, including its operating system, installed software, and files. These images can accumulate rapidly in size, especially when changes between snapshots are significant.

$$\text{New Storage Requirement} = \text{Original VM Size} + \sum (\text{Changes in Each Snapshot}) \qquad (6.1)$$

This equation demonstrates how each snapshot amplifies the total storage required to house the VM and its state history. Consequently, frequent snapshotting can lead to substantial storage consumption, necessitating careful management of snapshots and potential investment in additional storage solutions.

Another notable issue is the potential performance degradation associated with excessive snapshot usage.   Each snapshot layer introduces a small but cumulative overhead to file operations within the VM. This is because any read or write operation must traverse through the snapshot layers to ensure consistency and correctness. The overhead might be negligible for a few snapshots but can become significant with many layers, leading to perceptible slowdowns in VM performance.

Furthermore, reliance on snapshots for backup purposes is ill-advised.   Despite their utility in capturing the VM's state, snapshots do not replicate the security and redundancy of traditional backup solutions.   They reside on the same physical storage as the VM, meaning that any catastrophic failure affecting the primary storage would also compromise the snapshots.   For genuine data protection, external backups to separate physical or cloud storage are recommended.

- Snapshots increase storage requirements.

- Overuse of snapshots can degrade VM performance.

- Snapshots should not substitute for regular backups.

Additionally, managing snapshots requires a disciplined approach. Failure to maintain a clear organization or naming convention for snapshots can lead to confusion and difficulty in identifying appropriate rollback points. This can especially become a challenge in environments where multiple developers interact with the same VM or when snapshots are taken frequently without a consistent strategy.

A specific challenge in the context of Vagrant is ensuring that snapshots are correctly integrated with provisioning and configuration management tools. Changes made to the VM's configuration or software environment via external automation tools might not be fully captured by snapshots taken within Vagrant. Consequently, restoring a snapshot might not revert all aspects of the VM's state, particularly those aspects managed outside of Vagrant's scope.

Finally, it is essential to consider the limitations in Vagrant's native snapshot functionality when dealing with multi-machine environments. Vagrant's snapshot commands typically operate on a single VM at a time. Synchronizing snapshots across multiple VMs—ensuring that each VM's state corresponds to the same point in time—requires careful coordination and potentially custom scripting or tooling.

```
vagrant snapshot save [vm-name] snapshot-name
```

This command highlights the simplicity of snapshot creation in Vagrant for a single VM. Extending this functionality to handle complex multi-VM setups effectively requires additional efforts not inherently supported by Vagrant's snapshot mechanism.

In sum, while snapshots are a potent tool for managing VM states, their limitations demand respectful and judicious use. Balancing the advantages of snapshots against their potential downsides requires foresight, discipline, and sometimes creativity, ensuring they serve as an asset rather than a liability in development environments.

Chapter 7

Synced Folders and File Sharing

Synced Folders and File Sharing in Vagrant is a feature that enhances the workflow by enabling seamless file synchronization between the host machine and the virtual environment. This functionality is crucial for developers as it allows them to work in their preferred environment on the host machine while keeping the files automatically updated in the virtual machine, thereby simplifying the development and testing processes. Vagrant offers several mechanisms for sync, including default shared folders, NFS, rsync, and SMB, each with its own set of advantages and use cases. This chapter provides an overview of the available options, setup instructions, and tips for optimizing performance and usability, ensuring developers can make the most out of synced folders.

7.1   Overview of Synced Folders in Vagrant

Synced Folders in Vagrant facilitate a symbiotic file sharing mechanism between the host machine and the Vagrant guest machine. This feature is foundational to Vagrant's utility, bridging the gap between local development environments and isolated, virtual environments. By default, Vagrant shares your project directory (the one containing the Vagrantfile) with the virtual machine.

Vagrant's synced folder functionality supports various types of file synchronization, enabling developers to choose the most suitable method based on their project requirements.   The primary mechanisms include:

- Default Shared Folders: Utilizes VirtualBox's or VMware's default sharing system.

- NFS (Network File System): Offers better performance for larger projects or files.

- rsync: Ensures one-way synchronization with manual or automatic triggering.

- SMB (Server Message Block): Recommended for Windows hosts to improve performance and compatibility.

Configuring synced folders in Vagrant is straightforward. Modifications and specifications are typically made within the Vagrantfile, allowing for a high degree of customization. To specify a synced folder, you can use the `config.vm.synced_folder` method, which receives the path on the host machine, the path on the guest machine, and optionally, any type or additional options.

```
1  Vagrant.configure("2") do |config|
2     config.vm.box = "hashicorp/bionic64"
3
4     # Syncing a local directory with the guest /vagrant_data directory
5     config.vm.synced_folder "./host_data", "/vagrant_data"
6  end
```

This code snippet will synchronize the local `./host_data` directory with the `/vagrant_data` directory on the guest machine. The data will be kept in sync across both directories, reflecting any changes made on either side.

Understanding the underlying mechanics of each syncing method is crucial for optimizing the development and testing workflow. Each method, whether it be NFS, rsync, or SMB, comes with its own set of commands and configurations for initialization and operation. For instance, NFS requires proper setup on both the host and guest machines and may involve additional configuration for firewalls or network settings.

Additionally, performance considerations are vital when selecting a syncing mechanism. While NFS and SMB provide significant performance improvements over default shared folders, they may require additional setup and resources. Rsync offers unparalleled flexibility with its one-way synchronization, making it ideal for scenarios where constant, bi-directional syncing is not necessary.

Synced folders are a pillar of Vagrant's functionality, offering developers the flexibility to maintain a consistent and efficient workflow between their local and virtual environments. Through the appropriate configuration of synced folders, developers can ensure a seamless development process, leveraging the best of both the host and guest environments.

7.2 Configuring Synced Folders in the Vagrantfile

Configuring synced folders in Vagrant is accomplished by specifying configuration options within the `Vagrantfile`. The `Vagrantfile` is a Ruby script used to configure Vagrant environments. It allows for the definition of how the virtual machine (VM) is set up, including the configuration of synced folders. Synced folders enable files and directories to be shared between the host machine and the guest VM, ensuring that changes made in one location are mirrored in the other.

To set up a synced folder, the `config.vm.synced_folder` method is utilized within the `Vagrantfile`. This method requires two mandatory arguments: the path to the folder on the host machine and the path where it should be mounted on the guest machine. Additionally, it accepts a hash of options which can be used to fine-tune the behavior of the synced folder.

```
1  Vagrant.configure("2") do |config|
2    config.vm.synced_folder "./host/folder", "/guest/folder"
3  end
```

The above example demonstrates a basic configuration where `"./host/folder"` on the host is synced to `"/guest/folder"` on the guest VM. The path on the host machine is relative to the location of the `Vagrantfile`.

For more complex configurations and to utilize specific types of synced folders such as NFS, rsync, or SMB, additional options can be provided:

```
1  Vagrant.configure("2") do |config|
2    config.vm.synced_folder "./host/folder", "/guest/folder",
3                   type: "nfs",
4                   mount_options: ["rw", "vers=3", "tcp", "fsc" ,"actimeo=2"]
5  end
```

In this configuration, the `type` option specifies NFS as the syncing mechanism. The `mount_options` provides a list of options passed to the mount command, allowing for further customization.

It's important to note that each type of synced folder mechanism comes with its specific set of options and requirements.   For instance, using NFS requires the host to have NFS server installed and properly configured, which might not be the case on Windows hosts.

For projects requiring specific file permissions or where guest and host file permissions should be kept separate, the following options may be useful:

```
1  config.vm.synced_folder "./host/folder", "/guest/folder",
2                   owner: "www-data",
3                   group: "www-data"
```

This sets the owner and group of the files in the synced folder on the guest machine, which is particularly useful in web development scenarios where web servers expect certain permissions.

```
==> default: Mounting shared folders...
    default: /guest/folder => /path/to/host/folder
```

The output example above indicates the successful mounting of a shared folder. The host path is mapped to the specified guest path.

Careful consideration must be given to the selection and configuration of synced folders to avoid performance degradation, especially in large-scale projects. Certain types of synced folders may be more appropriate than others depending on the specific needs of the development environment and the performance characteristics of the host and guest operating systems.

Through the careful configuration of the `Vagrantfile`, developers can optimize their workflow by enabling efficient file synchronization between the host and guest machines.

7.3 Common Synced Folder Types: NFS, rsync, SMB

Let's discuss the various mechanisms Vagrant offers for syncing files between the host machine and the guest machines, namely NFS, rsync, and SMB. Understanding these mechanisms is crucial for selecting the most suitable option according to requirements such as performance, security, and convenience.

- **NFS (Network File System):** NFS is a distributed file system protocol that allows a user on a client machine to access files over a network in a manner similar to how local storage is accessed. Vagrant's support for NFS improves read/write performance significantly over the default synced folder system, especially beneficial for applications that read a large number of small files during startup.

To enable NFS, one must simply specify the `type` option in the `Vagrantfile` as shown below:

```
1   config.vm.synced_folder "host_folder/", "/guest_folder", type: "nfs"
```

Note that NFS requires administrative privileges to export the shared directory and may demand specific firewall or port settings to operate correctly. Moreover, while NFS offers substantial performance benefits, it does not support Windows hosts natively.

- **rsync:** rsync is another tool for synchronizing files and directories between two locations over a network. In Vagrant, rsync is particularly suited for one-time transfers or continuous synchronization with the `rsync-auto` command. Unlike NFS, rsync is compatible with Windows and offers a high degree of control over what gets synchronized via the inclusion or exclusion of files.

The basic syntax in the `Vagrantfile` for enabling rsync is:

```
1   config.vm.synced_folder "host_folder/", "/guest_folder", type: "rsync"
```

A notable limitation of rsync is the lack of real-time synchronization. Changes in the host directory are not automatically propagated to the guest machine; instead, synchronization occurs at the initiation of vagrant up, vagrant `reload`, or when manually triggered with vagrant rsync or vagrant rsync-auto.

- **SMB (Server Message Block):** SMB is a protocol for sharing files, printers, serial ports, and communications abstractions such as named pipes and mail slots between computers. Vagrant supports SMB shared folders on Windows hosts, providing a more performant and Windows-friendly alternative to NFS.

Configuration for SMB in the `Vagrantfile` looks like:

```
1   config.vm.synced_folder "host_folder/", "/guest_folder", type: "smb"
```

SMB setup requires user authentication for sharing directories, and Vagrant will prompt for the necessary credentials. One significant advantage of SMB over other sync methods is its support for automatic real-time synchronization.

In considering file synchronization options, the choice depends on factors such as the operating system of the host, desired performance characteristics, and whether real-time sync is crucial. NFS offers superior performance on non-Windows platforms, rsync provides flexibility and extensive customizability, while SMB presents an optimal solution for users on Windows seeking real-time synchronization. Understanding these options allows developers to tailor their development environment for maximum efficiency.

7.4 Performance Considerations for Synced Folders

When configuring synced folders in Vagrant, it is essential to deliberate on the performance implications associated with the various syncing methods offered. These methods, including the default shared folders, NFS, rsync, and SMB, impact the overall efficiency of file operations and can significantly influence the development experience depending on the size of the project, the frequency of file access, and the specific requirements of the development environment.

Firstly, it's crucial to understand that the default shared folder mechanism, while simple to set up, may not offer the best performance for all use cases. File access times can be slower, especially in large projects or where high I/O throughput is needed. This is primarily due to the overhead of managing file synchronization between the host and the guest machine within a virtualized environment.

```
1   # Example of setting up a default shared folder in Vagrantfile
2   config.vm.synced_folder ".", "/vagrant", type: "virtualbox"
```

Comparatively, NFS offers improved performance for file operations, making it a favored choice for scenarios requiring more intensive file

187

access. NFS reduces latency and increases throughput by leveraging the network file system protocol, which is particularly efficient over local networks.

```
1   # Example of setting up an NFS shared folder in Vagrantfile
2   config.vm.synced_folder ".", "/vagrant", type: "nfs"
```

Another option is rsync, which provides high performance by synchronizing files between the host and guest only when changes are detected. While this method can significantly reduce the overhead of file synchronization, it is not real-time and requires manual or scheduled syncing, potentially interrupting the development workflow.

```
1   # Example of setting up an rsync shared folder in Vagrantfile
2   config.vm.synced_folder ".", "/vagrant", type: "rsync"
```

Lastly, SMB is particularly useful for Windows environments, offering better performance over the default shared folders by using the Server Message Block protocol. However, SMB setup can be more complex and may require additional configuration on both the host and guest machines.

```
1   # Example of setting up an SMB shared folder in Vagrantfile
2   config.vm.synced_folder ".", "/vagrant", type: "smb"
```

To optimize performance, consider the following recommendations:

- For general-purpose development, NFS provides a good balance between ease of setup and performance improvement over the default shared folders.

- When developing on Windows, SMB may offer the best performance, provided the complexities of its setup can be managed.

- For projects requiring high I/O throughput, consider rsync for its efficiency in detecting and syncing only modified files.

- Regardless of the synchronization mechanism chosen, regularly monitor the performance impact on your development workflow and adjust configurations as necessary.

188

Furthermore, managing file permissions and ownership effectively can mitigate performance bottlenecks, as inappropriate settings might lead to unnecessary file access restrictions or delays.

```
$ chmod -R 755 /path/to/synced/folder
```

Conclusively, selecting the optimized file syncing strategy is contingent on the specific requirements of your project and development environment. By considering the characteristics of each syncing method and adhering to best practices for configuration and monitoring, you can significantly enhance the performance and efficiency of your development workflow using Vagrant's synced folders.

7.5 File Sharing Between Host and Guest Machines

File sharing between the host and guest machines in a Vagrant environment is a foundational aspect that significantly enhances productivity and workflow efficiency. This capability is designed to create a synchronized environment where changes made in one file system are reflected in the other, in real time or through manual synchronization processes.

To begin, it's essential to understand that Vagrant automatically sets up a synced folder. This folder shares the project directory (on the host) with the /vagrant directory inside the virtual machine. This default behavior facilitates immediate file sharing between your host machine and the virtual environment without additional configuration.

However, for more complex projects or specific workflow requirements, Vagrant provides several methods to configure file sharing, each with its nuances and setup procedures. Below, we delineate the primary methods available:

- **Default Shared Folders**: Utilizes VirtualBox's or VMWare's built-in sharing mechanisms. It's the simplest way to share

189

files but might not offer the best performance for large sets of files.

- **NFS (Network File System)**: Offers better performance than default shared folders, especially for high file count or size. It requires additional setup both in Vagrant and possibly on the host machine, depending on your operating system.

- **rsync**: Allows for manual synchronization of files between the host and guest machines. This method does not provide real-time sync but can be ideal for situations where bandwidth is limited, or changes do not need to be reflected instantly.

- **SMB (Server Message Block)**: Suitable for scenarios where the host is a Windows machine. SMB can offer better performance than some other options but requires more complex setup involving Windows networking features.

To configure these methods, one must understand the configuration options available in the Vagrantfile. Here is an example demonstrating how to set up NFS file sharing in a Vagrantfile:

```
1  Vagrant.configure("2") do |config|
2    config.vm.synced_folder ".", "/vagrant", type: "nfs"
3  end
```

This snippet tells Vagrant to use the NFS protocol for the synced folder, rather than the default VirtualBox shared folders mechanism. When the virtual machine is started with vagrant up, Vagrant will set up NFS to share the files.

One of the primary concerns with file sharing is ensuring consistency and performance. The choice of file sharing method can significantly impact the development workflow, as each has its advantages and peculiarities. For example, while NFS and SMB might offer better performance for larger projects, they require more setup and have specific OS dependencies. On the other hand, the default shared folders and rsync are easier to configure but might not meet the performance needs of all projects.

In practice, the best approach is often to start with the default shared folders for simplicity and then move to more advanced options like

NFS or SMB, as project complexity and performance requirements increase. It's also crucial to consider the development environment's specifics, such as the host and guest machine's operating systems, when choosing a file-sharing method.

Efficient file sharing between host and guest machines in Vagrant is pivotal for a seamless development experience. Understanding the various methods and how to configure them is essential for tailoring the development environment to specific project needs.

7.6 Bi-directional File Syncing

Bi-directional file syncing is a feature in Vagrant that enables changes made to files in either the host machine or the guest machine to be automatically replicated to the other side. This ensures that both environments always have the latest version of the files being worked on. This synchronicity is pivotal for developers who constantly modify files across both platforms but wish to avoid the cumbersome manual transfer of files.

To achieve bi-directional file syncing, Vagrant employs various mechanisms, each fitting different scenarios and performance needs. Understanding these mechanisms and their configuration is essential for optimal development workflows.

Configuring Bi-Directional Syncing

The primary method to configure bi-directional syncing is through the `Vagrantfile`. This configuration file dictates how Vagrant environments are set up, including the specifics of file syncing behavior. For bi-directional syncing, the type of synced folder must be chosen wisely to reflect the developer's needs.

```
1  config.vm.synced_folder "host_folder/", "/guest_folder", type: "rsync",
2    rsync__auto: true, rsync__exclude: ".git/"
```

The above snippet showcases an example where 'rsync' is used for syncing files. The `rsync__auto` option enables automatic syncing whenever files change on the host. However, it's important to note that changes made within the guest environment are not automatically synced back to the host with basic 'rsync'. For truly bi-directional syncing, a more sophisticated setup or a different synced folder type might be required.

Synced Folder Types for Bi-Directional Syncing

- **NFS:** Offers better performance compared to the default shared folders, especially for large files. However, it requires additional configuration on the host and does not support Windows hosts natively.

- **SMB:** Suitable for Windows hosts, SMB can provide bi-directional file syncing with adequate performance. SMB shares require additional setup, particularly on Linux guests.

- **VirtualBox Shared Folders:** This is the default option and offers seamless bi-directional syncing without additional configuration. However, it might lag in performance for extensive file operations.

Performance Considerations

When configuring bi-directional file syncing, performance is a critical consideration. Certain mechanisms may introduce latency or consume significant system resources during active development phases. It is crucial to balance the ease of setup and use with the performance implications of the chosen syncing mechanism.

For instance, NFS provides a notable performance increase over VirtualBox shared folders but requires manual setup steps on both the host and guest systems. Conversely, SMB might offer a good trade-off for Windows users, providing better performance without the complexity of NFS setup.

Bi-directional file syncing in Vagrant is a vital feature for developers looking to maintain a consistent working environment between their host and guest machines. By carefully selecting and configuring the appropriate syncing mechanism, developers can ensure a smooth, efficient workflow that minimizes manual file transfers and enhances productivity.

7.7 Managing File Permissions and Ownership

Managing file permissions and ownership is crucial when setting up synced folders in Vagrant, as it directly impacts the security and functionality of the development environment. This section will elaborate on how to effectively manage these settings to ensure smooth operation and data integrity between the host and the guest machines.

Permissions within synced folders dictate what actions can be performed on files and directories. These actions include reading, writing, and executing files, which are fundamental for development tasks. The ownership of these files and directories determines which users or groups can set these permissions. Incorrect settings can lead to inaccessible files or expose sensitive data.

Configuring these settings begins in the Vagrantfile, which allows specifying the owner, group, and permission mode for the synced folder. The syntax for configuring these attributes is presented below:

```
1  Vagrant.configure("2") do |config|
2    config.vm.synced_folder "host_folder/", "/guest_folder",
3    owner: "vagrant",
4    group: "www-data",
5    mount_options: ["dmode=775,fmode=664"]
6  end
```

In the above example, the owner and group options explicitly set the ownership of the synced folder to the user vagrant and the group www-data within the guest machine. The mount_options specify directory and file modes — in this scenario, directories are set to 775 and files to 664. This setup ensures that the owner and group have

full permissions, while others have only read or execute permissions,
enhancing security.

Adjusting file permissions and ownership might also necessitate
commands within the guest machine, especially when dealing with
complex projects or when initial settings need refinement. The
chown and chmod commands are typically employed for this
purpose:

```
1  chown -R vagrant:www-data /guest_folder
2  chmod -R 775 /guest_folder
```

The chown -R command recursively changes the owner and group
of the / guest_folder and its subdirectories to vagrant and www-data,
respectively. The chmod -R 775 command then recursively sets the
directory permissions to allow the owner and group to write, read,
and execute, while others can only read and execute.

Monitoring and diagnostics tools are sometimes required to audit file
permissions and ownership effectively. For Linux and Unix systems,
the ls -l command can be used to list files and directories with their
permissions, owner, and group, as shown in a typical output:

```
drwxrwxr-x 2 vagrant www-data 4096 Mar 10 10:00 guest_folder
```

This output displays the permissions (drwxrwxr-x), the number of
links (2), the owner (vagrant), the group (www-data), the size (4096
bytes), the modification date (Mar 10 10:00), and the directory name
(guest_folder).

In summary, managing file permissions and ownership in synced
folders is a dynamic process that requires careful planning and
ongoing maintenance to ensure a secure and functional
development environment. By leveraging the Vagrantfile
configuration options and employing standard Unix commands,
developers can effectively manage these settings to meet their
project's needs.

7.8 Syncing Strategy for Large Projects

Large projects often pose unique challenges when it comes to syncing files between the host machine and the virtual environment managed by Vagrant. These challenges can stem from the sheer volume of files, the complexity of the project's directory structure, and the necessity to maintain high performance and efficiency during synchronization. To navigate these challenges, a deliberate strategy tailored to the needs of large projects is essential.

First, consider the mechanism for file synchronization. While Vagrant offers various options such as NFS, rsync, and SMB, each comes with its own set of trade-offs in terms of speed, reliability, and setup complexity.

- NFS is known for better performance compared to the default shared folder system, especially for reading large numbers of files. However, it can be trickier to set up on Windows environments and might require additional software installation.

- Rsync provides a one-way synchronization from the host to the guest machine, which can be advantageous for projects where changes are made predominantly on the host side. Its initial setup can be simpler, but because it does not support real-time syncing, it might not be ideal for all use cases.

- SMB is generally recommended for Windows users and can offer performance benefits similar to NFS, but it can be less reliable on non-Windows hosts.

For large projects, developers should weigh these options carefully, considering the project's specific needs and the development team's workflow.

Using `Vagrantfile`, the configuration of synced folders can be optimized for large projects. Consider the following example that configures NFS for improved performance:

```
1  Vagrant.configure("2") do |config|
2    config.vm.box = "ubuntu/bionic64"
```

```
3
4      config.vm.synced_folder ".", "/vagrant", type: "nfs",
5          mount_options: ["rw", "vers=3", "tcp", "fsc" ,"actimeo=2"]
6    end
```

This configuration sets NFS as the sync method and includes several mount options to optimize performance:

- "rw" allows read and write permissions.

- "vers=3" specifies the NFS version to use, which can significantly affect performance.

- "tcp" ensures NFS uses the TCP protocol for improved reliability.

- "fsc" enables NFS file system caching, reducing the number of times files need to be reread from the network.

- "actimeo=2" sets the attribute cache timeout to 2 seconds, reducing latency in file operations.

For projects with a large number of files or directories, selectively syncing folders can further enhance performance. Only syncing the essential directories needed for development or testing minimizes the load on the syncing mechanism and reduces the risk of performance bottlenecks. This selective syncing can be configured in the Vagrantfile by specifying multiple synced_folder configurations, each with its own path and sync type as necessary.

Moreover, understanding and managing file permissions and ownership is crucial in large projects to ensure that the development environment in Vagrant mirrors the production environment closely. Inappropriate file permissions can lead to issues when running applications or services within the virtual machine. Vagrant allows for specifying the owner and group of synced folders through the :owner and :group options, respectively.

To efficiently handle large amounts of data and numerous files, a combination of the practices mentioned above is often necessary. It starts with choosing the right sync mechanism, optimizing configuration settings for performance, strategically selecting folders to sync, and correctly managing file permissions and ownership.   Together, these strategies form a comprehensive approach that can significantly improve the experience of working with large projects in Vagrant-environment setups.

7.9   Using Synced Folders for Development and Testing

Synced folders in Vagrant facilitate a seamless development and testing workflow by enabling real-time file synchronization between the host machine and the virtual environment.   This feature is particularly advantageous as it allows developers to utilize the tools and editors available on their host machine while simultaneously maintaining the up-to-dateness of files within the virtual machine (VM). Consequently, this setup mirrors the production environment closely, providing a high fidelity local development experience that is crucial for reliable software development and testing.

In order to effectively utilize synced folders for development and testing, it is essential to configure the `Vagrantfile` appropriately. This configuration acts as the central definition file for the project's VM, including settings for synced folders.   Within this file, developers specify the folders to sync, the syncing method, and any relevant options.

```
1  Vagrant.configure("2") do |config|
2    config.vm.box = "ubuntu/bionic64"
3
4    # Example of configuring a synced folder
5    config.vm.synced_folder "./host_folder", "/guest_folder"
6  end
```

This code snippet demonstrates the basic setup for a synced folder, linking a folder from the host machine ('./host_folder') to a corresponding folder within the VM ('/guest_folder').   Upon starting the VM with `vagrant up`, Vagrant ensures that these folders are synchronized according to the specified configuration.

Syncing methods such as NFS, rsync, and SMB offer different advantages, affecting file synchronization behavior and performance. For instance, NFS is known for better performance compared to the default sync method, particularly for projects with a large number of files. The choice of syncing mechanism can have a significant impact on the responsiveness and speed of the development environment, especially when dealing with web applications that require frequent asset compilation or large databases.

To leverage synced folders for testing, it is advisable to place the application's source code within a synced folder. This setup allows for immediate reflection of changes made on the host in the VM, facilitating rapid iterative testing without the need for manual file transfers or complex deployment steps. Configuring continuous integration tools or automated test suites within the VM to watch these folders for changes can further streamline the testing process, enabling a seamless transition from development to testing.

```
1  # Example of using rsync for a synced folder
2  config.vm.synced_folder "./host_app", "/guest_app", type: "rsync",
3    rsync__exclude: ".git/"
```

In this example, the rsync method is employed to sync the application folder, excluding the .git directory to optimize synchronization speed and prevent unnecessary transfers. It is a common practice to exclude version control directories, log files, or temporary files from syncing to enhance performance.

Synced folders not only simplify the development and testing cycle but also ensure that the environment within the VM remains consistent with the host. This consistency is vital for reducing "works on my machine" issues, leading to more predictable and reliable software deployments.

Managing file permissions and ownership within synced folders is an additional aspect to consider, particularly when multiple users are involved or when specific permissions are required for the application to function correctly in the VM. Vagrant provides options within the synced_folder configuration to manage these aspects, ensuring that the development and testing environment adheres to the necessary security and access controls.

Using synced folders in Vagrant for development and testing offers a flexible and efficient approach to software development. By enabling seamless synchronization between the host and VM, developers can utilize their preferred tools and workflows while ensuring that their code remains consistent with the testing and production environments. Proper configuration and optimization of synced folders can significantly enhance the development experience, streamline testing processes, and lead to more reliable software outcomes.

7.10 Troubleshooting Synced Folder Issues

Synced folder issues in Vagrant can range from minor annoyances to significant obstacles that hinder development workflows. Identifying and resolving these problems requires a systematic approach. This section will explore common troubleshooting steps for resolving issues related to synced folders in Vagrant environments.

Firstly, it's imperative to verify the basic configuration settings in the `Vagrantfile`. Incorrect or missing configurations are often the root cause of synchronized folder issues. The following is a typical synced folder configuration snippet:

```
1   config.vm.synced_folder "host/directory", "/guest/directory"
```

Ensure the paths specified are correct and accessible. The host directory path must exist on your physical machine, and the guest directory path should reflect a valid location within the virtual machine.

If configurations appear correct but files are still not syncing, investigate the specific type of synced folder mechanism being utilized (e.g., NFS, rsync, SMB). Each method has unique requirements and potential pitfalls.

- **NFS** can cause issues related to file permissions or NFS server configuration errors. Check the NFS server status on the host machine and verify that necessary firewall ports are open.

- **rsync** problems often stem from rsync not being installed on

the host or guest machine, or from missing rsync paths in the
Vagrantfile. Install rsync where missing and ensure paths are
correctly specified.

- **SMB** issues frequently relate to authentication errors or SMB
  version mismatches between the host and guest. Verify SMB
  settings and credentials.

Performance issues with synced folders might not point to an
outright failure but can significantly impact development velocity.
When facing performance degradation, consider the following
optimizations:

```
1   config.vm.synced_folder ".", "/vagrant", type: "nfs", :mount_options => ["
        actimeo=2"]
```

This configuration employs NFS with a custom option to reduce attribute caching time, potentially improving performance.

Monitoring logs provides insightful information for troubleshooting.
Vagrant and the underlying virtualization provider (e.g., VirtualBox,
VMware) generate detailed logs that can highlight errors or warnings
related to file synchronization. Access Vagrant logs by increasing the
verbosity level of the output:

```
1   vagrant up --debug
```

For VirtualBox, log files can be found within the VirtualBox VMs
folder, usually located in the home directory of the host machine.

Lastly, issues with synced folders can sometimes be resolved by resetting the state of the Vagrant environment. This can be accomplished
by halting the virtual machine and restarting it:

```
1   vagrant halt
2   vagrant up
```

If problems persist, consider destroying the virtual environment and
recreating it. Note that this will remove any data not stored in synced
folders or other persistent storage mechanisms:

```
1   vagrant destroy
2   vagrant up
```

Troubleshooting synced folder issues in Vagrant involves checking configurations, understanding the specifics of the sync method in use, utilizing performance optimizations, examining logs for errors, and, as a last resort, resetting or recreating the Vagrant environment. By systematically working through these steps, most synced folder issues can be resolved efficiently.

7.11 Advanced Techniques: Custom Syncing Solutions

In some development scenarios, the standard syncing solutions provided by Vagrant - namely NFS, rsync, and SMB - might not meet all the specific requirements. Therefore, understanding how to implement custom syncing solutions becomes essential for tailoring the development environment to exact needs. This section will discuss creating custom sync scripts, leveraging third-party tools, and integrating these solutions into the Vagrant environment effectively.

Firstly, it is important to comprehend the mechanism Vagrant uses to synchronize files. At its core, Vagrant initializes and maintains a connection between the host and guest machines, allowing files to be shared and synced. The customization of this process involves two primary steps: the creation of a custom script and the modification of the Vagrantfile to utilize this script.

```
1   # Sample custom sync script (sync.sh)
2   #!/bin/bash
3   # Custom script to sync files from host to guest
4   rsync -avz --delete /path/to/host/folder/ vagrant@192.168.33.10:/path/to/guest/
        folder
```

The script above uses rsync to synchronize files from the host to the guest machine. It specifies the source folder, the destination (along with the guest machine's IP address), and additional flags to control the sync behavior. This basic example can be expanded with more complex logic, such as selective sync, error handling, or notification mechanisms for successful syncs.

Integrating the custom script into the Vagrantfile involves using the `trigger` functionality, which Vagrant provides for hooking custom actions into the VM lifecycle events like up, halt, and reload. The following example demonstrates how to execute the custom sync script every time the VM is started:

```
1   Vagrant.configure("2") do |config|
2     # Other configurations
3
4     config.vm.define "my_vm" do |my_vm|
5       my_vm.trigger.before :up do |trigger|
6         trigger.name = "Syncing files..."
7         trigger.run = {path: "./sync.sh"}
8       end
9     end
10  end
```

In addition to creating custom scripts, several third-party tools can be leveraged to facilitate file syncing. Tools like Unison offer the capability for bi-directional file syncing, which can be particularly helpful in development environments where changes are frequent and need to be propagated instantly in both directions. Incorporation of these tools follows a similar approach - scripting the sync process and triggering it within the `Vagrantfile`.

```
1   # Example usage of Unison for bi-directional syncing
2   unison /path/to/host/folder ssh://vagrant@192.168.33.10//path/to/guest/folder
```

The command above initiates a bi-directional sync using Unison. This example assumes that SSH keys have been set up for seamless authentication between the host and guest machines.

When implementing custom syncing solutions, several considerations must be taken into account:

- **Performance:** Custom solutions can introduce significant overhead if not optimized properly. It is crucial to evaluate the performance impact and adjust the syncing frequency and scope accordingly.

- **Security:** Ensuring secure transmissions (e.g., using SSH for rsync) is fundamental to protect the data shared between the host and the guest.

- **Error Handling:** The custom script should include robust error handling to deal with sync failures gracefully.

- **Flexibility:** The solution should be flexible enough to accommodate changes in the development environment, such as new dependencies or directory structures.

To summarize, while Vagrant provides versatile options for file syncing, advanced projects may require custom solutions for enhanced flexibility and performance. By following the methodology outlined above - scripting the sync process, using the trigger mechanism in the Vagrantfile, and optionally leveraging third-party tools - developers can create tailored syncing solutions that perfectly fit their project's unique requirements.

7.12 Best Practices for File Sharing with Vagrant

File sharing with Vagrant is an indispensable feature for developers looking to maintain consistency between their local development environment and the virtual machine. To achieve an efficient and trouble-free file synchronization process, it is important to adhere to several best practices. These guidelines are designed to optimize performance, ensure security, and facilitate a smooth workflow.

- **Selective Synchronization:**

  Synchronize only the directories necessary for your project. This can be done by specifying particular folders in the Vagrantfile. Limiting the scope of synced folders reduces the overhead, leading to better performance.

```
1   config.vm.synced_folder "./host_folder", "/guest_folder"
```

  This command syncs the "./host_folder" from your host machine to "/guest_folder" in the virtual machine.

- **Utilize NFS for macOS and Linux Hosts:**

203

When working on macOS or Linux, opting for NFS can significantly improve the speed of file transfers compared to the default sync method. Configure NFS by adding an additional parameter to your synced folder configuration.

```
1    config.vm.synced_folder "./host_folder", "/guest_folder", type: "
        nfs"
```

- **Leverage rsync for One-way Sync Needs:**

  If your workflow requires only a one-way file sync from the
  host to the guest, rsync is an efficient choice. It reduces the
  overhead by preventing continuous file watch operations,
  enhancing performance.

```
1    config.vm.synced_folder "./host_folder", "/guest_folder", type: "
        rsync"
```

  Remember to manually trigger synchronization with `vagrant`
  `rsync` or `vagrant rsync-auto` for continuous syncing.

- **Optimize SMB Usage in Windows:**

  On Windows hosts, SMB may provide better performance than
  the default sync option. Be mindful to configure SMB correctly,
  ensuring you have the necessary permissions and network configurations.

```
1    config.vm.synced_folder "./host_folder", "/guest_folder", type: "
        smb"
```

- **Managing File Permissions and Ownership:**

  Correctly managing file permissions and ownership is crucial,
  particularly when sharing files between environments with
  varying permission models. Vagrant allows the adjustment of
  ownership and permissions within the Vagrantfile.

```
1    config.vm.synced_folder "./host_folder", "/guest_folder",
        mount_options: ["dmode=777","fmode=666"]
```

This setting configures the directory mode to 777 and the file
mode to 666 to avoid permission issues.

- **Continuous Monitoring for Changes:**

  Use tools like `vagrant rsync-auto` for rsync to automatically monitor for file changes and synchronize in real-time. This ensures that your virtual environment is always up-to-date with the host.

  ```
  $ vagrant rsync-auto
  ```

- **Exclude Unnecessary Files:**

  Excluding non-essential files and directories can significantly enhance performance. Use the `rsync__exclude` option to ignore specific files or directories during synchronization.

```
1   config.vm.synced_folder "./host_folder", "/guest_folder",
2       type: "rsync", rsync__exclude: [".git/", "node_modules/"]
```

- **Upgrade Vagrant and Virtualization Software:**

  Always keep Vagrant and your virtualization software (e.g., VirtualBox, VMWare) up-to-date. Updates often include performance enhancements, bug fixes, and new features that can improve file synchronization.

- **Investigate and Resolve Syncing Conflicts Promptly:**

  In case of file syncing discrepancies or issues, promptly investigate and resolve these conflicts. Early detection can prevent more significant problems in the future and ensure a smooth development process.

- **Utilize Vagrant's Plugin Ecosystem:**

  Explore Vagrant's extensive plugin ecosystem for additional tools that can optimize your file syncing process. Plugins can offer customized solutions to specific file sharing needs or performance optimizations.

Following these best practices will help in achieving an efficient, secure, and reliable file sharing setup between your host machine and the Vagrant-managed virtual machines. Proper configuration and maintenance of synced folders are key to a productive development environment.

Chapter 8

Customizing and Extending Vagrant

Customizing and Extending Vagrant opens up a wealth of possibilities for tailoring development environments to meet the specific needs of a project or team. Beyond its core functionality, Vagrant can be augmented with plugins, custom scripts, and integrations with other tools to enhance its capabilities, ranging from network configurations to provisioning and automation tasks. Whether you're looking to integrate cloud services, improve workflow automation, or create entirely new functionality, Vagrant's extensible architecture allows for significant flexibility. This chapter explores how to leverage Vagrant's plugin system, write custom plugins, and utilize community resources to extend Vagrant far beyond its out-of-the-box capabilities, providing a pathway for developers and teams to craft their ideal development environment.

8.1　Customizing the Vagrant Environment

Customizing the Vagrant environment is an essential skill for developers who seek to tailor their development settings to meet the project requirements accurately or aim to enhance the overall workflow. Vagrant, by design, offers a high degree of customization through its configuration file, typically named `Vagrantfile`. This file uses Ruby's syntax to configure settings related to the base box, network, synced folders, and provisioners. We will discuss each of these components in detail to enlighten how they can be customized to refine development environments effectively.

Configuring the Base Box

The base box is a fundamental component in Vagrant, serving as the starting point for any Vagrant environment. It represents a pre-packaged development environment that includes an operating system and potentially other software or configurations. Developers have the freedom to choose from a wide array of publicly available boxes or create custom ones. To specify a base box in a `Vagrantfile`, the following syntax is used:

```
1  Vagrant.configure("2") do |config|
2    config.vm.box = "hashicorp/bionic64"
3  end
```

This code snippet sets the base box to "hashicorp/bionic64", a popular box containing a minimal installation of Ubuntu 18.04 LTS.

Network Configuration

Network settings are pivotal for defining how the Vagrant environment interacts with the outside world. These settings can be tailored to establish port forwarding, private networks, or public networks, allowing customization of network access and enhancing development workflows that depend on specific networking requirements. For instance, to configure port forwarding from the host to the guest machine, the following configuration can be added:

```
1  Vagrant.configure("2") do |config|
2    config.vm.network "forwarded_port", guest: 80, host: 8080
3  end
```

This setup forwards traffic from port 8080 on the host machine to port 80 on the guest machine, facilitating web server testing directly from the host.

Synced Folders

Synced folders establish a shared directory between the host and the guest machine, making it seamless to work on project files without having to worry about transferring files between the two environments. By default, Vagrant syncs the project directory (where the Vagrantfile resides) to /vagrant within the guest machine. This behavior can be customized or extended as shown below:

```
1  Vagrant.configure("2") do |config|
2    config.vm.synced_folder "./host_folder", "/guest_folder"
3  end
```

This line changes the default synced folder path, ensuring that the host directory ./host_folder is synced with /guest_folder on the guest machine.

Provisioning

Provisioning tools automate the process of configuring and setting up the software within a Vagrant environment after its initial creation. Vagrant supports various provisioning mechanisms, including shell scripts, Chef, Puppet, and Ansible, allowing developers to incorporate automation into their development setup seamlessly. A simple shell script provisioner could look like this:

```
1  Vagrant.configure("2") do |config|
2    config.vm.provision "shell", inline: <<-SHELL
```

```
3        apt-get update
4        apt-get install -y nginx
5      SHELL
6    end
```

This snippet automates the installation of Nginx on the guest machine by using a shell script provisioner, showcasing how developers can automate their environment setup processes.

The discussed customization options represent a fraction of what's achievable within Vagrant's ecosystem. By leveraging these configurations, developers can sculpt a development environment that perfectly aligns with their project's demands, ultimately increasing productivity and consistency across development teams.

8.2   Extending Vagrant with Plugins

Extending the functionality of Vagrant involves the utilization of plugins, which are self-contained pieces of code designed to augment the capabilities of Vagrant by offering new commands, features, and settings. Understanding how to leverage plugins is crucial for developers seeking to customize their Vagrant environments beyond the default provision.

Discovering Available Plugins

To start, it is essential to identify the plugins that could enhance your Vagrant environment. The Vagrant community has developed numerous plugins for a wide range of purposes, from simplifying network configurations to integrating with cloud service providers. The primary resource for discovering available plugins is the official Vagrant plugin repository, which can be accessed via the Vagrant website or through community forums and directories.

```
1    vagrant plugin search <plugin-name>
```

This command searches the Vagrant plugin repository for a plugin that matches the specified <plugin-name>. It returns a list of plugins, including brief descriptions and version numbers, helping users to make informed decisions about which plugins to install.

Installing Plugins

Once a desirable plugin has been identified, it can be installed using the Vagrant plugin management system. The general format for installing a Vagrant plugin is as follows:

```
1  vagrant plugin install <plugin-name>
```

Upon execution, Vagrant downloads and installs the plugin, making its functionality available immediately. It is advisable to review the plugin documentation, as some plugins may require additional configuration steps or dependencies to function correctly.

Configuring Plugins

Configuration of plugins typically occurs within the Vagrantfile, allowing for seamless integration into the provisioning workflow. Each plugin may introduce its own set of configuration options, which can be specified using the Vagrant.configure interface. For example, configuring a hypothetical vagrant-network plugin to modify network settings might look like this:

```
1  Vagrant.configure("2") do |config|
2    config.vm.network.plugin "vagrant-network", {
3      ip: "192.168.33.10",
4      netmask: "255.255.255.0"
5    }
6  end
```

This block demonstrates how to call upon the vagrant-network plugin within the Vagrantfile, passing a hash of configuration options to tailor the network setup of the Vagrant environment.

211

Creating and Sharing Custom Plugins

For developers who seek to create their own plugins, Vagrant offers a robust framework for plugin development. This involves creating a RubyGem, which is a package containing the plugin code, and adhering to the Vagrant plugin API for compatibility. Detailed instructions and examples are provided in the Vagrant documentation, guiding developers through the process of developing, testing, and distributing their plugins.

In summary, plugins offer a powerful means to extend and customize the Vagrant environment to suit specific requirements. Whether installing existing plugins, configuring them to meet precise needs, or developing new ones, the flexibility provided by the Vagrant plugin system significantly enhances the development workflow, facilitating a more efficient and productive process.

8.3   Writing Your Own Vagrant Plugin

To begin writing your own Vagrant plugin, an understanding of the Vagrant ecosystem and Ruby programming language is essential. Vagrant plugins are written in Ruby and distributed as RubyGems, thus familiarity with Ruby and its gem packaging system provides a solid foundation for plugin development.

First, install the necessary Ruby development tools if you haven't already. This typically involves setting up Ruby on your system and installing the bundler gem, which is crucial for managing a Ruby project's dependencies.

```
1  gem install bundler
```

Once the development environment is prepared, start by creating a new directory for your plugin and navigate into it. Initialize a new RubyGem project within this directory.

```
1  bundle gem vagrant-myplugin
2  cd vagrant-myplugin
```

This command generates the basic structure for a new RubyGem, including a Gemfile for dependency management and a .gemspec file for specifying gem metadata.

The next step involves adding Vagrant as a dependency in your plugin's .gemspec file. Open the vagrant-myplugin.gemspec file in your preferred text editor and add the following line:

```
1  spec.add_dependency "vagrant", ">= 2.0"
```

This specifies that your plugin requires Vagrant version 2.0 or newer. It is important to ensure compatibility with the version of Vagrant your plugin targets to avoid unexpected behavior.

Now, create the main plugin file inside the lib directory. This is where the core logic of your plugin will reside. Vagrant plugins follow a specific structure, typically starting with a module that matches your plugin's name. For instance, for a plugin named vagrant-myplugin, you would start with:

```
1   module VagrantMyPlugin
2     class Plugin < Vagrant.plugin("2")
3       name "My Vagrant Plugin"
4
5       command "mycommand" do
6         require_relative "path/to/command"
7         MyCommand
8       end
9     end
10  end
```

This basic structure defines a new plugin with a custom command. The command method within the plugin class registers a new command named mycommand, which points to a class handling the command's execution. The require_relative call specifies the relative path to the Ruby file containing this class, typically located within the same lib directory.

As for implementing the command, create a new Ruby file at the specified path and define a class inheriting from Vagrant.plugin(2, :command). This class should implement two methods: execute and initialize as shown below:

```
1  module VagrantMyPlugin
2    class MyCommand < Vagrant.plugin("2", :command)
```

```
 3
 4      def initialize(app, env)
 5        super
 6        # Initialization code here
 7      end
 8
 9      def execute
10        # Command logic here
11        @env.ui.info("Hello from My Vagrant Plugin!")
12      end
13    end
14  end
```

The execute method is where the main functionality of your command is implemented. The example above prints a simple message
to the console. This method has access to the @env instance variable,
which contains information about the current Vagrant environment
and allows interaction with the Vagrant UI.

After completing the plugin development, build and install your gem
locally to test it with Vagrant.

```
1  gem build vagrant-myplugin.gemspec
2  vagrant plugin install ./vagrant-myplugin-0.1.0.gem
```

Finally, test your plugin by running the custom command you've
registered with Vagrant.

```
vagrant mycommand
```

The output should display the message defined in your execute
method, indicating that your plugin is working as intended.

8.4   Integrating   Vagrant   with   Cloud
Providers

Integrating Vagrant with cloud providers enables users to
instantiate and manage virtual machines (VMs) in a cloud
environment directly from Vagrant. This capability is particularly
useful for development teams who need to replicate production
environments closely or utilize resources that are not available

locally. This section will discuss how to integrate Vagrant with popular cloud providers, such as AWS, Google Cloud, and Azure, through the use of specific plugins and configurations.

Firstly, it is essential to understand that Vagrant itself does not inherently support cloud providers out of the box. To integrate Vagrant with a cloud provider, you must install the appropriate plugin. For example, for AWS, the vagrant-aws plugin is required. These plugins extend Vagrant's functionality, allowing it to interact with the cloud provider's APIs and manage resources accordingly.

```
1  # Installation of the AWS plugin
2  vagrant plugin install vagrant-aws
```

After installing the necessary plugin, the next step involves configuring your Vagrantfile to specify the provider and include the necessary configurations such as access keys, secret keys, instance types, and regions.

```
1   Vagrant.configure("2") do |config|
2     config.vm.box = "dummy"
3     config.vm.provider :aws do |aws, override|
4       aws.access_key_id = "YOUR_ACCESS_KEY"
5       aws.secret_access_key = "YOUR_SECRET_KEY"
6       aws.instance_type = "t2.micro"
7       aws.region = "us-east-1"
8       override.ssh.username = "ubuntu"
9     end
10  end
```

It is crucial to replace "YOUR_ACCESS_KEY" and "YOUR_SECRET_KEY" with your actual AWS credentials. The dummy box acts as a placeholder since the actual VM instance will be created in the AWS cloud, instead of locally.

Similar configurations apply when integrating with other cloud providers, although the specific settings and provider name will vary. Here is an example for Google Cloud Platform using the vagrant-google plugin:

```
1  # Installation of the Google plugin
2  vagrant plugin install vagrant-google
```

```
1  Vagrant.configure("2") do |config|
2    config.vm.box = "google/gce"
```

215

```
3    config.vm.provider :google do |google, override|
4      google.google_project_id = "YOUR_PROJECT_ID"
5      google.google_json_key_location = "PATH_TO_YOUR_JSON_KEY"
6      override.ssh.username = "gce_user"
7    end
8  end
```

In each case, after configuring the Vagrantfile appropriately, you can use the usual Vagrant commands to manage your VM instances in the cloud. For instance, vagrant up will create and start a VM instance in the specified cloud environment, vagrant ssh allows you to connect to it, and vagrant destroy will terminate the instance.

```
$ vagrant up --provider=aws
$ vagrant ssh
$ vagrant destroy
```

Integrating Vagrant with cloud providers greatly enhances its utility by bridging the gap between local development environments and cloud-based resources. This allows for more flexible and scalable development practices, making it possible to easily test and deploy applications in an environment that closely mimics production setups.

It is recommended to refer to the official documentation of each plugin for more detailed information on configuration options and additional functionalities. Additionally, ensure that you are aware of the costs associated with running instances on the cloud provider to avoid unexpected charges.

This section highlighted the process for integrating Vagrant with major cloud providers, showcasing the ease with which developers can extend the reach of their local development environments to the cloud. The subsequent sections will delve into other customization and extension possibilities within Vagrant environments.

8.5   Custom Box Creation and Distribution

Creating a custom Vagrant box involves packaging a specific environment setup that can be easily distributed and reused across different machines and projects. This process encompasses the creation of a base virtual machine (VM), configuring it according to requirements, and then packaging it into a Vagrant box file. This section delineates the step-by-step procedure for creating custom Vagrant boxes and methods for their distribution.

Preparation of the Base Virtual Machine

The initial step in creating a custom box is to prepare a base VM. This involves selecting a virtualization software (e.g., VirtualBox, VMware) and installing an operating system (OS) of choice on the VM. During the OS installation and VM setup, remember to:

- Install the minimum required software for the VM to function. This includes the OS itself, SSH server, and any other essential tools or packages.

- Configure a single main user with sudo or administrative privileges.

- Ensure that the VM acquires an IP address through DHCP to simplify network configurations.

Upon completion of the VM preparation, it is vital to perform a cleanup process to reduce the final box size and remove sensitive information. This cleanup may include:

- Clearing the history of the shell, logs, and temporary files that were created during the setup process.

- Defragmenting the disk space and zeroing out free space to improve compression.

Packaging the Virtual Machine

With the base VM prepared and cleaned, the next stage is packaging it into a format understood by Vagrant. This process converts the VM into a .box file. To package the VM, execute the following Vagrant command:

```
1  vagrant package --base <NAME_OF_VM>
```

In the command, replace <NAME_OF_VM> with the name of the VM as identified within the virtualization software. This command generates a file named package.box, which represents the custom Vagrant box.

Distributing the Custom Box

After generating the .box file, the final step involves making the box available for use, either for personal use across projects or for sharing with others. There are multiple venues for distribution:

- **Local Distribution:** A simple method where the .box file is copied directly to other machines or shared through internal networks.

- **Vagrant Cloud:** Hosting the box on Vagrant Cloud (formerly known as Atlas) allows users to download and use the box with a simple Vagrantfile configuration. To upload a box to Vagrant Cloud, create an account, upload the box file, and provide a unique name for the box.

- **HTTP Server:** Boxes can also be distributed by hosting them on a standard HTTP server. This method requires that the URL of the .box file be specified in the Vagrantfile.

Once distributed, the custom box can be initialized by specifying its name or URL in a Vagrantfile:

```
1  Vagrant.configure("2") do |config|
2    config.vm.box = "<BOX_NAME_OR_URL>"
3  end
```

Replace <BOX_NAME_OR_URL> with the name of the box on Vagrant Cloud or the URL where the box file is hosted. This configuration ensures that anyone using the Vagrantfile pulls the correct custom environment, simplifying development workflows and environment setup.

8.6 Using Vagrant to Manage Containerized Environments

Containerization has become an essential strategy in software development, enabling applications to run reliably when moved from one computing environment to another. By coupling Vagrant with container technologies such as Docker or Kubernetes, developers can streamline the workflow and achieve a higher degree of environment consistency. This enhanced workflow is vital for reducing the "it works on my machine" syndrome and ensuring that applications run smoothly in different environments.

Integrating Vagrant with Docker

Docker has emerged as the standard for containerization, offering an ecosystem for developing, shipping, and running applications. Vagrant's built-in support for Docker allows it to manage the lifecycle of Docker containers directly.

Getting Started with Docker as a Provider

To use Docker as a provider, one must first ensure that both Vagrant and Docker are installed on the development machine. The next step involves defining a Vagrantfile that specifies Docker as the provider.

```
1  Vagrant.configure("2") do |config|
2    config.vm.provider "docker" do |d|
3      d.image = "ubuntu:latest"
4    end
5  end
```

In this Vagrantfile, we specify Docker as the provider and use the "ubuntu:latest" image as the base for our container. This simple example lays the foundation for launching Docker containers through Vagrant.

Customizing Docker Containers

Beyond simply starting containers, Vagrant allows for customization of Docker environments through various configuration options.

```
1  Vagrant.configure("2") do |config|
2    config.vm.provider "docker" do |d|
3      d.image = "python:3.8-slim"
4      d.name = "my_python_app"
5      d.has_ssh = false
6      d.ports = ["5000:5000"]
7      d.volumes = ["/host/path:/container/path"]
8    end
9  end
```

In this configuration, we're specifying a Python image, setting a container name, disabling SSH (as it might be unnecessary), mapping ports for web applications, and sharing volumes between the host and the container.

Leveraging Kubernetes with Vagrant

For more complex applications, particularly those that run across multiple containers, Kubernetes provides a powerful orchestration platform. While Vagrant does not support Kubernetes directly as a provider, it can initiate and manage Kubernetes clusters using tools like Kubeadm or Minikube.

Creating a Kubernetes Cluster with Minikube

Minikube is a tool that makes it easy to run Kubernetes locally. Vagrant can be used to create a VM that runs Minikube, providing a straightforward path to Kubernetes development.

```
1  Vagrant.configure("2") do |config|
2    config.vm.box = "generic/ubuntu1804"
3    config.vm.provision "shell", inline: <<-SHELL
4      curl -Lo minikube https://storage.googleapis.com/minikube/releases/latest/
               minikube-linux-amd64
5      chmod +x minikube
6      sudo mv minikube /usr/local/bin/
7      minikube start --driver=none
8    SHELL
9  end
```

This script uses Vagrant's shell provisioner to download Minikube, make it executable, move it to a suitable location, and finally start a Kubernetes cluster with Minikube. The '–driver=none' flag tells Minikube to run Kubernetes directly on the host without creating an additional VM, which is suitable for this use case since Vagrant is already creating a VM.

Using Vagrant to manage containerized environments significantly simplifies the development and deployment process. By integrating with Docker, developers can harness the simplicity and speed of container management. Meanwhile, for applications that require multi-container orchestration, Vagrant's ability to manage VMs makes it an excellent tool for running Kubernetes locally. With these tools, Vagrant extends its utility beyond mere virtual machine management, embracing the container revolution and making it accessible to developers.

8.7 Automating Development Environment Setup

Automating the setup of development environments reduces manual configuration efforts and ensures a consistent, reproducible environment across different machines. This includes the automation of installing software, configuring settings, and preparing the system for use. Vagrant, combined with provisioning tools like Ansible, Puppet, or Shell scripts, provides an efficient pathway for achieving this automation.

Using Provisioners with Vagrant

Vagrant supports automated provisioning through several built-in provisioners. These provisioners can execute scripts, install and configure software, or even apply complex configurations to the guest machine after it has been created and booted.

- Shell provisioners execute shell scripts.

- Ansible provisioners allow for Ansible playbooks to be run.

- Puppet provisioners enable the application of Puppet manifests.

- Chef provisioners can apply Chef cookbooks.

To automate the development environment setup, select a provisioner that best fits the project's needs and configure it within the Vagrantfile.

Example: Automating with Shell Provisioner

A common approach for automating the development environment setup is using the shell provisioner due to its simplicity and directness. Below is a sample Vagrantfile configuration snippet that demonstrates how to use the shell provisioner to install Apache on a Ubuntu guest machine.

```
1  Vagrant.configure("2") do |config|
2    config.vm.box = "ubuntu/bionic64"
3
4    config.vm.provision "shell", inline: <<-SHELL
5      sudo apt-get update
6      sudo apt-get install -y apache2
7    SHELL
8  end
```

Upon running vagrant up, Vagrant will initialize the virtual machine based on the "ubuntu/bionic64" box, and then automatically execute the specified shell commands to install Apache.

Benefits of Environment Setup Automation

Automating the setup of development environments offers several advantages:

- **Consistency:** Ensures every team member is working in an identical environment, reducing "it works on my machine" situations.

- **Efficiency:** Saves time by eliminating the need for manual setup and configuration.

- **Scalability:** Facilitates easy replication and distribution of environments across multiple machines.

- **Version Control:** Allows environment setup scripts to be version-controlled along with application code, improving collaboration and traceability.

Extending Provisioning with Community Scripts

The Vagrant community has contributed many provisioning scripts and configurations for various development environments. Exploring community resources such as GitHub repositories or Vagrant's own Vagrant Cloud can provide ready-made solutions and inspirations for automating development environment setup.

To integrate community scripts, include them in the Vagrantfile using the appropriate provisioner syntax. For shell scripts, GitHub Gist URLs can be directly used with the `shell` provisioner's `path` option, enabling the execution of remote scripts.

Automating the setup of development environments simplifies the initial configuration process, ensures consistency across team members' environments, and significantly reduces setup times. By utilizing Vagrant's built-in provisioners, such as the shell provisioner, and leveraging community resources, developers can achieve highly tailored and automated development environments.

8.8　Leveraging　Vagrant　in　Continuous Integration

Continuous Integration (CI) stands as a cornerstone in the realm of agile software development, aiming to merge all developers' working copies to a shared mainline several times a day. The integration of Vagrant into CI processes can significantly enhance the consistency and reliability of builds by encapsulating the development environment. This section will dissect the methods and best practices for integrating Vagrant into CI workflows, highlighting the value it brings to streamlining development pipelines.

Vagrant's utility in CI is predicated on its ability to create and manage identical development environments across different stages of the software development lifecycle. This consistency is crucial in eliminating the "it works on my machine" syndrome, a common challenge in software development that occurs when code works in a developer's environment but fails in others. By ensuring that the development, testing, and production environments are mirrored, Vagrant mitigates the risk of discrepancies that can lead to unexpected behaviors or bugs.

To integrate Vagrant within a CI pipeline, consider the following steps:

1. **Version Control Integration**: Ensure that the Vagrant configuration files (`Vagrantfile` and provisioning scripts) are version-controlled along with the application code. This practice ensures that any changes to the environment setup are tracked and can be reverted if necessary.

2. **Automated Environment Provisioning**: Use Vagrant's provisioning capabilities to automatically set up the test environment as part of the CI pipeline. This step typically involves executing a `vagrant up` command, which reads the `Vagrantfile` to create and configure the virtualized environment according to the specifications.

3. **Running Tests**: With the environment provisioned, run the application's test suite. This step can be automated using CI tools such as Jenkins, Travis CI, or GitLab CI, invoking commands within the Vagrant environment to execute the tests.

4. **Environment Teardown**: After the tests are completed, it's essential to clean up resources to avoid wasting computational resources or interfering with subsequent builds. This is achieved through the vagrant destroy command, which removes the created virtual machines.

The integration of Vagrant into the CI process can be further illustrated through an example CI pipeline configuration for a Jenkins job:

```
pipeline {
    agent any
    stages {
        stage('Provision Vagrant Environment') {
            steps {
                sh 'vagrant up'
            }
        }
        stage('Run Tests') {
            steps {
                sh 'vagrant ssh -c "cd /vagrant && ./run_tests.sh"'
            }
        }
        stage('Destroy Vagrant Environment') {
            steps {
                sh 'vagrant destroy -f'
            }
        }
    }
}
```

This Jenkins pipeline script outlines a basic three-stage process: environment provisioning, test execution, and environment teardown. The vagrant up command initializes the environment, followed by executing a script (run_tests.sh) inside the Vagrant machine that runs the application's tests. Finally, the environment is destroyed to release resources.

- Advantages:

225

- Ensures consistency across development, testing, and pro-
    duction environments.

- Streamlines the development pipeline by automating en-
    vironment setup and teardown.

- Facilitates parallel testing and development workflows.

- Challenges:

  - Initializing and destroying VMs can introduce additional
      time to the CI pipeline.

  - Requires additional disk space for storing VM images.

  - May necessitate learning Vagrant-specific configurations
      and commands.

While integrating Vagrant into CI pipelines may introduce some
initial setup and learning curve, the benefits in terms of
environment consistency, reliability, and automation far outweigh
these challenges. As development teams strive for more efficient
and error-free software delivery, the role of tools like Vagrant in CI
processes will undoubtedly grow more significant.

8.9   Security in Customized Vagrant Environ-
ments

When deploying and maintaining Vagrant environments, especially
those that are customized or extended with additional plugins and
scripts, security considerations become paramount. An improperly
secured environment can expose sensitive data, become a vector for
attacks, or compromise the integrity of the development process. In
this context, we will focus on best practices for securing Vagrant
environments, covering aspects such as network configurations,
box sourcing, plugin management, and shared folder usage.

Network Configurations and Port Forwarding:

Vagrant provides extensive networking features, which, if not configured properly, can open up vulnerabilities. To ensure secure network configurations, consider the following:

- Use private networking options wherever possible. This restricts network access to the host machine and trusted devices.

- Limit port forwarding to only those ports that are essential for development, and avoid opening unnecessary ports to the host machine or the wider network.

- Regularly audit the Vagrantfile for any network configurations that might inadvertently expose services to the public internet.

Box Sourcing and Management:

Vagrant boxes serve as the foundation of Vagrant environments. Securing these is crucial:

- Only download boxes from trusted sources. Preferably, use boxes published by well-known organizations or those that are officially verified by HashiCorp.

- Regularly update boxes to ensure that they contain the latest security patches. Configure Vagrant to check for box updates automatically.

- Consider building custom boxes for greater control over the security posture of your base images.

Plugin Security:

Plugins extend Vagrant's functionality but can also introduce security risks:

```
$ vagrant plugin list
```

- Audit installed plugins regularly using the command above to verify their necessity and integrity.

- Remove any unused or outdated plugins to minimize the attack surface.

- Review plugin source code, when available, or rely on plugins that have a strong community backing and are actively maintained.

Managing Shared Folders:

Shared folders create a bridge between the host and the guest machine, which can be exploited if not properly secured:

- Limit shared folders to those that are absolutely necessary for development purposes.

- Use Vagrant's synced folder options to set appropriate permissions, ensuring that sensitive files on the host are not inadvertently exposed to the guest machine.

- Regularly audit the permissions and contents of shared folders to ensure that they do not contain sensitive information that could be compromised.

Continuous Security Assessment:

To maintain a strong security posture, perform continuous assessments of your Vagrant environments:

Regularly update the Vagrant software and plugins to their latest versions.

$$(8.1)$$

Implement automated security scanning tools to detect vulnerabilities early. Regularly review Vagrant configurations and scripts for potential security improvements.

Securing customized Vagrant environments requires diligent management of network configurations, box sourcing, plugin usage, and shared folders. By adhering to the best practices outlined above and committing to continuous security assessment, developers can significantly mitigate the risks associated with Vagrant-based development workflows.

8.10 Performance Optimization for Custom Vagrant Setups

Performance optimization in a customized Vagrant environment is a critical aspect that directly impacts the efficiency and responsiveness of the development workflow. This section will discuss strategies to enhance Vagrant's performance, focusing on resource allocation, Vagrant box optimization, usage of synced folders, and efficient networking configurations.

Resource Allocation

Optimal allocation of resources such as CPU and RAM to the Vagrant virtual machines (VMs) plays a pivotal role in performance. It is essential to balance the resources between the host machine and the VM to avoid overallocation, which could lead to the host system becoming unresponsive or slow. Vagrantfile provides the capability to configure these settings. For instance, to allocate 2 CPUs and 4GB RAM to a VM, the following configuration can be used:

```
1  config.vm.provider "virtualbox" do |v|
2    v.customize ["modifyvm", :id, "--cpus", "2"]
3    v.customize ["modifyvm", :id, "--memory", "4096"]
4  end
```

It is recommended to experiment with different configurations to find the most suitable setup that ensures smooth operation of both the host system and VMs.

Optimizing Vagrant Boxes

The choice of Vagrant box can significantly influence the performance of the development environment. It is advisable to use lean, minimal boxes that contain only the essential components required for the development work. Customizing and trimming down the installed packages and services in the Vagrant box can reduce boot times and overall resource consumption.

Synced Folders

Vagrant's synced folders feature allows for easy sharing of files between the host system and the VM. However, the default syncing mechanism can be slow, especially in large projects with numerous files. Switching to NFS (Network File System) or Rsync can improve the speed of file synchronization. Here is how NFS can be enabled:

```
1   config.vm.synced_folder ".", "/vagrant", type: "nfs"
```

Note that NFS might require additional configurations on the host and guest systems, and its support varies depending on the host operating system.

Networking Configurations

Improper networking setups can lead to performance bottlenecks. Using private networks instead of port forwarding can provide better performance for applications that require network communication between the host and VMs. A private network can be configured as follows:

```
1   config.vm.network "private_network", type: "dhcp"
```

This configuration enhances performance by creating a direct network connection between the host and the VM, eliminating the overhead associated with NAT (Network Address Translation) and port forwarding.

Additional Measures

- **Vagrant Caching**: Utilizing caching plugins, such as vagrant-cachier, can reduce provisioning times by caching packages and other files. - **Disabling GUI**: Unless necessary, disabling the GUI of VMs can free up system resources. - **Parallel Execution**: For multi-machine setups, consider enabling parallel execution to speed up the Vagrant provisioning process.

```
1   config.vm.box = "hashicorp/precise64"
2   config.vm.provision :shell, :inline => "echo hello"
```

In essence, optimizing performance in custom Vagrant setups requires careful consideration of resource allocation, choice of Vagrant boxes, efficient file synchronization methods, networking configurations, and leveraging additional performance enhancement measures. Applying these strategies can significantly improve the responsiveness and efficiency of Vagrant environments, leading to a more productive development experience.

8.11   Debugging Custom Vagrant Setups

Debugging custom Vagrant setups is a critical skill for identifying and resolving issues within development environments. This involves scrutinizing Vagrantfiles, interacting with the Vagrant CLI, examining log files, and utilizing debugging flags effectively. The aim is to quickly pinpoint the root cause of a problem and apply appropriate solutions to maintain the efficiency and reliability of the development workflow.

Firstly, understanding the structure and syntax of the Vagrantfile is fundamental. Errors here can lead to Vagrant behaving unexpectedly. Syntax errors, misconfigurations, or incompatible settings between various components configured in the Vagrantfile can all lead to issues. Employing a systematic approach by validating the Vagrantfile through online validators or Vagrant's built-in validation commands can quickly identify syntax-related issues.

```
1   vagrant validate
```

This command checks for any syntax errors or misconfigurations in your Vagrantfile, providing feedback on how to rectify them.

Another critical aspect is leveraging Vagrant's logging capabilities. Increasing the verbosity of the logs can reveal intricate details about the operations being performed and where they might be failing.

231

This is particularly useful when dealing with provisioning scripts or plugin interactions.

```
1   VAGRANT_LOG=debug vagrant up
```

The VAGRANT_LOG environment variable adjusts the log level. The debug level provides extensive details, which can be instrumental in identifying the failure point in the setup process.

Provisioning scripts are common culprits of issues in custom Vagrant environments. It's crucial to ensure that these scripts are idempotent and fail gracefully. Logging within the provisioning scripts themselves can also provide valuable insights into their execution flow.

```
1   echo "Starting the provisioning script..."
2   # Your provisioning commands go here
3   echo "Provisioning script completed."
```

Enclosing provisioning commands with log statements in the script can help trace the execution progress and identify where issues occur.

Networking misconfigurations can lead to Vagrant machines being unable to communicate with each other or the host. Utilizing Vagrant's network troubleshooting commands can aid in diagnosing these issues.

```
1   vagrant ssh -c "ping -c 4 8.8.8.8"
```

This command, executed from the host machine, uses Vagrant's SSH capability to run a ping command inside the Vagrant machine, testing its external connectivity.

Finally, the Vagrant community and documentation are invaluable resources. Many common problems and their solutions have been documented either in the official Vagrant documentation or by the community. Engaging with the community through forums or GitHub issues can also provide specific solutions to uncommon problems.

Debugging custom Vagrant setups necessitates a comprehensive understanding of Vagrant's workings, a methodical approach to problem-solving, and effective use of the available diagnostic tools and resources. By following these strategies, developers can ensure their Vagrant environments are robust and resilient against a wide variety of issues.

8.12 Community and Resources for Vagrant Customization

Vagrant's versatility and widespread adoption can largely be attributed to its vibrant community and the plethora of resources available for customization and extension. Whether a novice seeking guidance on the basics or an experienced user aiming to tailor sophisticated development environments, the community and resources surrounding Vagrant offer invaluable support and inspiration.

Official Documentation: The cornerstone for any Vagrant user is its comprehensive official documentation. Available on the Vagrant website, the documentation meticulously details everything from installation, getting started guides, to advanced features like networking and boxes management. This resource is regularly updated to reflect the latest features and use cases, making it a reliable source of information.

GitHub Repository: The Vagrant GitHub repository not only hosts the source code but serves as a hub for reporting issues, contributing to the codebase, and exploring pull requests. Users can contribute to the ongoing development of Vagrant, propose new features, or fix bugs, fostering a collaborative environment for improvement.

Vagrant Plugins Directory: Extending Vagrant's functionality often involves the use of plugins. The Vagrant plugins directory is a curated list of available plugins contributed by the community. It allows users to discover new plugins, understand their functionalities, and learn how to install and configure them to suit their needs.

Community Forums and Q&A Sites: Platforms like Stack Overflow and the official Vagrant community forums are replete with discussions, solutions, and advice on various Vagrant-related topics. These forums are an excellent place for seeking help with specific problems, sharing knowledge, and staying informed about best practices and the latest trends in Vagrant usage.

Vagrant Cloud: Vagrant Cloud is a service provided by HashiCorp, the creators of Vagrant. It facilitates the sharing of Vagrant boxes, allowing users to publish and discover boxes for a wide range of use cases. Vagrant Cloud is an invaluable resource for finding base boxes or sharing custom boxes with the community.

Blogs and Tutorials: Numerous tech blogs and tutorial sites offer in-depth articles, how-tos, and series on Vagrant. These resources can provide practical insights into real-world applications of Vagrant, from basic setups to complex, multi-machine environments. Blogs and tutorials complement the official documentation by offering diverse perspectives and innovative uses of Vagrant.

Conferences and Meetups: Vagrant, being part of the broader DevOps and software development community, often features in conferences and meetups. These gatherings present opportunities to learn from experts, discover the latest developments, and network with other Vagrant users. Many conferences also offer workshops or sessions specifically focused on Vagrant.

Contributing to Vagrant: For those looking to give back to the community, contributing to Vagrant can be a rewarding experience. Contributions are not limited to code. Users can contribute through writing documentation, reporting bugs, improving translations, and providing feedback on new features.

In summary, the wealth of community and resources for Vagrant customization underscores the tool's flexibility and the collaborative spirit of its user base. By leveraging these resources, developers can greatly enhance their Vagrant setups, streamline their development processes, and contribute to the collective knowledge and capabilities of the Vagrant community.

Chapter 9

Debugging and Troubleshooting

Debugging and Troubleshooting are critical skills when working with Vagrant as they enable users to quickly identify and resolve issues within their virtual development environments. Despite its design to streamline development workflows, challenges such as networking problems, provisioning errors, or configuration missteps can arise. Understanding how to effectively leverage Vagrant's built-in tools and logs for diagnosing issues is crucial for maintaining a smooth and efficient development process. This chapter delves into common Vagrant problems, offering step-by-step guides for troubleshooting, techniques for debugging configurations and provision scripts, and tips for preventing common issues, ensuring users can resolve problems swiftly and keep their projects on track.

9.1   Introduction to Debugging in Vagrant

Debugging in Vagrant is an essential skill that every developer needs to possess to ensure their development environments run smoothly. Unlike traditional software development where issues often pertain to code alone, Vagrant introduces complexities related to virtualization, networking, and integration with various provisioning tools. The initial step towards effective debugging in Vagrant starts with a thorough understanding of how Vagrant operates, including its interaction with virtual machine (VM) providers like VirtualBox, VMware, etc., and provisioners such as Ansible, Puppet, or Shell scripts.

Vagrant operates by creating and configuring virtual development environments based on a Vagrantfile. This file acts as the blueprint for your environment, specifying the base box to use, configurations, network settings, synced folders, and provisioning scripts. Debugging complexities often arise from misconfigurations or compatibility issues within this file or the environments it interacts with.

The process of debugging can be broadly categorized into several steps:

- **Identifying the problem:** This involves observing the symptoms of the issue. For example, an error during vagrant up could indicate problems with the base box, Vagrantfile configurations, or connectivity issues with the VM provider.

- **Isolating the cause:** Once the general area of the problem is identified, further investigation is needed to isolate the cause. This may involve testing with different configurations, examining log files, or using Vagrant's built-in debugging commands.

- **Resolving the issue:** With the cause identified, the next step is to apply a solution. This might involve editing the Vagrantfile, updating tools or dependencies, or changing network settings.

- **Preventing future occurrences:** Finally, consider what steps can be taken to prevent a similar issue from happening again. This could include adding additional checks or documentation or implementing a more robust testing process.

Vagrant provides several tools and commands to aid in debugging, the most notable being its detailed log output and the --debug flag which can be added to most Vagrant commands to produce verbose diagnostic output. Here is an example of using the --debug flag:

```
1  vagrant up --debug
```

The output from running a command with --debug can be extensive, providing a deep insight into the operations Vagrant is performing. It can reveal interactions with the VM provider, the execution of provisioning scripts, and detailed error messages. Here is a simplified example of part of a debug log output:

```
DEBUG subprocess: Waiting for process to exit. Remaining to timeout: 32000
DEBUG subprocess: Exit status: 0
 INFO interface: info: Machine booted and ready!
```

Understanding Vagrant's logging and output is crucial for diagnosing and debugging issues efficiently. This includes knowing which logs to consult, how to interpret the output, and when to utilize increased verbosity to uncover hidden issues. Additionally, familiarity with the common pitfalls within the provisioning process, network configuration, and synced folders can save considerable time and frustration.

Mastering debugging in Vagrant is not merely about fixing problems as they arise but developing a comprehensive understanding of how Vagrant environments are constructed, configured, and operated. With this knowledge, developers can minimize disruptions to their workflow and maintain productive development environments.

9.2   Common Vagrant Issues and How to Resolve Them

In this section, we will discuss several common issues encountered by users of Vagrant, alongside precise resolutions. The focus will be on areas such as connectivity, provisioning, and configuration, which are frequently cited sources of frustration. By understanding these common stumbling blocks, users can more quickly identify and resolve issues, leading to a smoother development experience.

Connectivity Issues

One of the frequent challenges with Vagrant involves connectivity problems, particularly in scenarios involving forwarded ports or private networks. Such issues can manifest as an inability to access services running within the Vagrant environment from the host machine or vice versa.

To resolve connectivity issues related to forwarded ports, verify the configuration in the `Vagrantfile`. Specifically, ensure that the `config.vm.network` directive is correctly set up to forward the appropriate ports. For example:

```
1  config.vm.network "forwarded_port", guest: 80, host: 8080
```

This configuration forwards traffic from port 8080 on the host to port 80 on the guest. If services are still inaccessible, checking the firewall settings on both the host and guest machines is recommended, as these can often block intended connections.

Provisioning Errors

Provisioning errors commonly occur when configuring the virtual machine with scripts or configuration management tools. Errors might stem from syntax mistakes, incorrect assumptions about the base environment, or issues with external resources such as package repositories or files expected to exist in certain locations.

When encountering a provisioning error, the first step is to review the output provided by Vagrant during the provisioning process. This output often includes error messages that can provide clues about the nature of the problem. For more detailed information, enabling more verbose output or debugging mode in the provisioning tool being used is often helpful. For instance, when using shell scripts for provisioning, adding a -x option to the shebang line will increase the verbosity:

```
1  #!/bin/bash -x
```

Configuration Missteps

Misconfigurations in the `Vagrantfile` can lead to a broad range of issues, from the virtual machine failing to boot, to incorrect networking configurations, or errors related to synced folders. Frequently, such missteps are due to incorrect syntax or misunderstanding the configuration options available.

To troubleshoot configuration issues, starting with a minimal `Vagrantfile` and incrementally adding configuration settings can help isolate the problematic configuration. Vagrant's documentation provides comprehensive details on the configuration options available, which should be consulted to ensure options are correctly applied.

For instance, if a synced folder is not behaving as expected, ensuring the configuration matches the syntax as specified in the documentation can be a good starting point:

```
1  config.vm.synced_folder "./host_folder", "/guest_folder"
```

Preventing Common Issues

While troubleshooting is an essential skill, preventing issues before they occur can vastly improve the development experience.

Adhering to best practices such as keeping the `Vagrantfile` version-controlled, documenting custom configurations or provisioning steps, and regularly updating Vagrant and provider software can preempt many common problems.

Additionally, leveraging the Vagrant community's wealth of knowledge through forums or official documentation can provide insights and prevent known issues from recurring in your development environments.

In summary, understanding these common issues along with their resolutions can significantly reduce the time spent troubleshooting Vagrant environments, allowing for a more productive and less frustrating development process.

9.3 Debugging   Vagrant   Networking Problems

Debugging networking problems in Vagrant is a common challenge that can hinder the development workflow, especially when virtual environments do not communicate as expected. This section will discuss several methods for diagnosing and resolving networking issues within Vagrant environments.

Firstly, verifying the network configuration in the Vagrantfile is crucial. This file contains settings that dictate how your virtual machines (VMs) are networked. There are several networking options available in Vagrant, including private networks, public networks, and forwarded ports. An incorrect setting can lead to connectivity issues.

```
1  Vagrant.configure("2") do |config|
2    config.vm.network "private_network", ip: "192.168.50.4"
3  end
```

The above code snippet illustrates how to configure a private network with a specific IP address. Ensure the IP address does not conflict with other devices on your network.

Next, testing connectivity directly from the host to the Vagrant VM is a straightforward approach to troubleshooting networking issues. Use the `ping` command to test connectivity. If `ping` fails, there is likely a problem with the network configuration or connectivity.

```
PING 192.168.50.4 (192.168.50.4): 56 data bytes
64 bytes from 192.168.50.4: icmp_seq=0 ttl=64 time=0.369 ms
```

After confirming network connectivity, inspecting the VM's network settings from within the VM is another critical step. Use commands like `ifconfig` (on Unix-like systems) or `ipconfig` (on Windows) to view the VM's IP configuration. Compare this information with the configuration specified in the Vagrantfile to identify discrepancies.

If connectivity issues persist, examine the firewall settings on both the host and the guest VM. Firewalls can block network traffic, resulting in connectivity problems. Ensure that the necessary ports are open and that no rules are blocking the expected traffic.

- On Unix-like systems, use `iptables` to examine and modify firewall rules.

- On Windows, use the `Windows Firewall` interface to check for any blocking rules.

Additionally, Vagrant's built-in networking troubleshooting commands can provide insights into networking configurations and potential problems. The `vagrant reload` command can be used to restart the VM and apply any changes made to the network settings in the Vagrantfile. Sometimes, a simple restart can resolve networking issues.

For more complex networking scenarios, such as bridged networking or multiple VMs needing to communicate, understanding the underlying virtualization provider's networking capabilities is essential. For example, if using VirtualBox, the VirtualBox Manager GUI provides detailed network information and settings that can be adjusted to resolve connectivity problems.

In summary, resolving networking problems in Vagrant environments requires a step-by-step approach to diagnose and correct issues. Starting from checking the Vagrantfile configuration, testing direct connectivity, inspecting VM network settings, checking firewall configurations, and understanding the virtualization provider's networking features are all crucial steps in troubleshooting Vagrant networking problems.

9.4   Troubleshooting Provisioning Errors

Troubleshooting provisioning errors in Vagrant environments requires a systematic approach to identify and resolve the underlying issues. Provisioning errors can occur for various reasons, including syntax errors in provisioning scripts, incorrect configurations, missing dependencies, and incompatibilities between the provisioning tools and the operating system of the VM. This section examines common provisioning errors and provides detailed steps to diagnose and fix them.

One of the first steps in troubleshooting is to ensure that the provisioning script is syntactically correct. For Shell scripts, this can be done by running the script manually on a VM that mirrors the Vagrant environment.

```
1   # Shell script syntax check
2   bash -n script.sh
```

If the syntax check returns an error, the output will indicate the line number and the nature of the error, simplifying the debugging process.

```
script.sh: line 42: unexpected EOF while looking for matching `''
```

Another frequent source of provisioning errors is missing dependencies or packages that the script expects to be present on the system. This issue can be resolved by updating the script to include commands for installing any required packages before proceeding with other operations. Here is an example for a script that ensures the installation of git before attempting to clone a repository.

```
1  # Ensure git is installed
2  sudo apt-get update && sudo apt-get install -y git
3
4  # Clone a repository
5  git clone https://github.com/example/repo.git
```

Incorrect configuration files can also lead to provisioning errors. It is essential to verify that all paths, permissions, and settings within the provisioning scripts are correct for the target environment. For instance, attempting to copy files to a non-existent directory on the VM will result in an error. To avoid such issues, you can add checks or create the necessary directories before file operations.

```
1  # Create directory if it doesn't exist
2  mkdir -p /usr/local/example
3
4  # Copy files
5  cp /vagrant/data/config /usr/local/example/config
```

Incompatibilities between provisioning tools or scripts and the VM's operating system version can also cause provisioning failures. Ensuring compatibility often requires checking the documentation of the provisioning tool for supported operating systems and versions, then comparing this information with the VM's OS details. The following command can be used to retrieve the operating system version information:

```
1  # Check operating system version
2  cat /etc/os-release
```

```
PRETTY_NAME="Ubuntu 20.04 LTS"
```

For more complex issues, Vagrant's verbose mode can be helpful in diagnosing provisioning errors. This mode outputs detailed logs of the provisioning process, making it easier to pinpoint the step where the error occurs.

```
1  # Run Vagrant with verbose provisioning
2  vagrant up --provision --debug
```

Finally, it's advisable to consult the documentation of the specific provisioning tool being used. Most tools have their troubleshooting guides that address common errors and their resolutions.

243

By following these steps, developers can systematically diagnose and resolve most provisioning errors encountered in Vagrant environments. Additionally, maintaining best practices such as version control for provisioning scripts and regularly testing the provisioning process in clean environments can help prevent errors and ensure a smooth development workflow.

9.5 Diagnosing Synced Folder Issues

Synced folder issues in Vagrant are often notable for causing confusion and frustration during the development phase. These problems usually manifest as files not being properly shared between the host and the guest machine, leading to inconsistencies and unexpected behavior in the development environment. Precision in identifying and resolving synced folder issues is therefore indispensable for maintaining an efficient workflow.

The root causes of these issues can range from incorrect configuration settings to compatibility problems with the host or guest filesystems. In this section, steps for diagnosing and resolving common synced folder issues will be elaborated upon.

- Verify the Configuration: The first step involves ensuring that the configuration in the `Vagrantfile` is correctly set up for synced folders. The configuration directive should resemble the following:

```
1   config.vm.synced_folder "host\_directory/", "/guest\_directory"
```

Ensure the paths specified are accessible and correct. An improper path can lead to the folder not being synced as expected.

- Filesystem Permissions: Filesystem permission issues can prevent files from being shared between the host and the guest. It's critical to verify that the user within the guest machine has the required permissions to access the synced folders. Adjustments can be made either in the Vagrant configuration or within the guest machine to rectify permission issues.

- Provider-specific Issues: Depending on the provider (VirtualBox, VMware, etc.), there might be provider-specific issues affecting the synced folders. For example, VirtualBox shared folders have known performance issues with large numbers of files. Reviewing provider-specific documentation and forums can unveil solutions tailored to these peculiarities.

- Use of NFS or SMB: For performance improvements or to circumvent compatibility issues, using NFS (Network File System) for Linux/Mac hosts or SMB (Server Message Block) for Windows hosts may provide a solution. Configuration for NFS or SMB can be done in the Vagrantfile as follows:

```
1  config.vm.synced_folder "host\_directory/", "/guest\_directory", type: "
       nfs"
```

Note that using NFS or SMB might require additional setup on the host system, such as installing NFS server tools or configuring SMB sharing.

- Vagrant and Version Control Systems: When working with Version Control Systems (VCS) such as Git, ensure that line-ending configurations do not cause file changes that would disrupt the sync process. This can be adjusted in the VCS configuration.

Diagnosing synced folder issues effectively requires a methodical approach, starting from the most common causes to more complex scenarios. In instances where the above steps do not resolve the problem, consulting the log files generated by Vagrant can provide insights into underlying issues. The vagrant up and vagrant reload commands can be appended with the --debug flag to obtain verbose output that could point towards the source of the problem:

```
1  vagrant up --debug
```

This debug output can be extensive; therefore, focusing on sections of the log pertaining to synced folders is advisable.

To summarize, successfully diagnosing and resolving synced folder issues in Vagrant involves a combination of verifying configurations, checking permissions, considering provider-specific limitations, potentially utilizing NFS or SMB, and being mindful of interactions with version control systems. By following these guidelines, developers can ensure that their development environments remain coherent and synchronized across the host and guest machines.

9.6   Understanding Vagrant's Logging and Output

Vagrant provides a multi-level logging system designed to offer insights into the internal operations of Vagrant processes, making it an invaluable tool for debugging. The logging output from Vagrant can be categorized into two main types: standard output and debug-level logs. Understanding how to effectively interpret and use these logs is paramount in identifying and resolving issues within a virtual development environment.

Standard Output   Standard output in Vagrant is the immediate feedback provided to the user upon executing various Vagrant commands such as vagrant up, vagrant halt, or vagrant reload. This output typically includes information about the state transitions of the virtual machine (VM), such as booting up, shutting down, or reloading, as well as any initial errors encountered during these processes.

For instance, during the execution of vagrant up, the user might see the following output indicating a successful operation:

```
Bringing machine 'default' up with 'virtualbox' provider...
==> default: Importing base box 'ubuntu/trusty64'...
==> default: Matching MAC address for NAT networking...
==> default: Setting the name of the VM: project_default_1415203131234_45678
==> default: Clearing any previously set forwarded ports...
...
```

This output is crucial for understanding the general state and progress of the VM's operations. However, it may not always provide in-depth detail about errors or issues.

Debug-Level Logs For more detailed troubleshooting, Vagrant offers an expanded logging mode known as debug mode. This mode can be enabled by appending the --debug flag to any Vagrant command, e.g., vagrant up --debug. Debug mode yields extensive output that covers the internal workings of Vagrant, including interactions with providers like VirtualBox, VMware, etc., internal state changes, and detailed error messages.

The inclusion of debug-level logs is instrumental when standard output does not provide enough context or detail about an issue. For example, if vagrant up fails with a non-descriptive error message, running vagrant up --debug might reveal detailed information about the specific operation that failed, which can help in diagnosing the problem more effectively.

It is important to note that debug output can be voluminous and might include sensitive information. As such, when sharing debug logs on public forums or with support teams, it is advisable to review and sanitize the logs appropriately.

To illustrate, a segment of a debug log might look like this:

```
DEBUG subprocess: Waiting for process to exit. Remaining to timeout: 32000
DEBUG virtualbox_6_1:    - [1, "dhcpserver", "add", "--netname",
 "HostInterfaceNetworking-
VirtualBox Host-Only Ethernet Adapter #2", "--ip", "10.10.10.1",
 "--netmask", "255.255.255.0",
"--lowerip", "10.10.10.3", "--upperip", "10.10.10.254", "--enable"]
DEBUG subprocess: Exit status: 0
```

Debug logs not only offer a granular view of each step that Vagrant undertakes but also indicate how external dependencies impact these processes.

Interpreting Logs When interpreting Vagrant's logging and output, it is crucial to identify the stage at which an error occurs and the specific components involved. Standard output is often sufficient for identifying configuration errors or issues during the VM's lifecycle transitions. In contrast, debug-level logs are more suited for dissecting intricate problems that require an understanding of Vagrant's interactions with underlying technologies.

Both types of logs can indicate common issues such as synchronization errors, networking misconfigurations, or provider-specific problems. By carefully analyzing this output, developers can efficiently diagnose problems, leading to quicker resolution times and less downtime in development environments.

Conclusively, mastering the interpretation of Vagrant's logs and output is indispensable for effective debugging. With practice, developers can leverage these tools to maintain high productivity levels and ensure the reliability of their virtual development environments.

9.7   Using Vagrant's Debug Mode

Vagrant's debug mode is an invaluable tool for users seeking to understand the inner workings of their virtual development environments or to troubleshoot issues that arise during the setup and use of Vagrant. This mode increases the verbosity of output generated by Vagrant commands, providing detailed information that can aid in identifying the source of problems.

To enable debug mode, the VAGRANT_LOG environment variable must be set to the "debug" level before executing a Vagrant command. This can be done through the command line in most operating systems. For instance, in a UNIX-like terminal, the command would appear as follows:

```
1  VAGRANT_LOG=debug vagrant up
```

This command initiates the Vagrant environment startup process with debug-level logging enabled, offering a granular view of each step undertaken by Vagrant. It is important to note that the debug output will be extensive, covering everything from internal Vagrant operations to interactions with providers like VirtualBox, VMware, etc.

The output of the debug mode is directed to the standard output (stdout) by default. Depending on the terminal or shell environment, it may be beneficial to redirect this output to a file for easier inspection and analysis. To achieve this redirection, the command could be modified as follows:

```
1  VAGRANT_LOG=debug vagrant up > vagrant_debug_log.txt 2>&1
```

The redirection of standard output (stdout) and standard error (stderr) to a file named vagrant_debug_log.txt facilitates a more accessible review process. Users can search through the log file using text editor features or command-line tools like grep to locate specific error messages or operational details.

When analyzing the debug logs, users should look for entries that indicate errors, such as those starting with "ERROR", or warning messages that might suggest suboptimal configurations or potential issues. Additionally, logs provide insights into the execution flow of provision scripts, network setup procedures, and synced folder operations, among other aspects of the Vagrant environment.

It is crucial to unset the VAGRANT_LOG environment variable or set it to a less verbose level once the necessary information has been gathered and the debugging session is complete. Continuously running Vagrant in debug mode can significantly slow down operations and produce unwieldly log files that are difficult to manage. To revert to the default logging level, the following command can be used:

```
1  unset VAGRANT_LOG
```

Or, alternatively, the environment variable can be redirected to "info" or another less verbose level suitable for regular operations:

```
1  VAGRANT_LOG=info
```

Mastering the use of Vagrant's debug mode is pivotal for development and operations professionals working with Vagrant environments. By providing a comprehensive view of the actions undertaken by Vagrant, debug mode assists in pinpointing issues, understanding the cause of unexpected behavior, and refining configurations to ensure a smooth development workflow.

9.8   Resolving Performance Issues

Resolving performance issues in Vagrant involves understanding the underlying causes that can lead to slow performance or resource bottlenecks in virtual development environments.   Performance degradation can manifest in various forms, such as prolonged boot times for Vagrant boxes, sluggish response times during development activities, or excessive CPU or memory usage that impacts the host machine's overall performance.   This section aims to provide systematic approaches to identify and resolve these performance-related issues, ensuring an optimized development workflow.

Firstly, it's essential to pinpoint the root cause of the performance issue. Vagrant environments are influenced by several factors, including but not limited to the Vagrant box being used, the configuration settings defined in the `Vagrantfile`, the resources allocated to the virtual machine, and the host system's performance characteristics.

Analyzing Resource Allocation

A common cause for performance issues pertains to inadequate resource allocation. By default, Vagrant assigns a conservative amount of resources to virtual machines to ensure compatibility across various host systems.   However, these defaults may not suffice for all development environments, particularly those requiring substantial computational power or memory.

Reviewing and adjusting the configuration settings in the `Vagrantfile` can often address resource-related performance issues. For example, increasing the amount of memory or CPUs allocated to the virtual machine can significantly enhance performance:

```
1  config.vm.provider "virtualbox" do |v|
2    v.memory = 4096
```

```
3    v.cpus = 2
4    end
```

It's crucial, however, to allocate resources within the host's capacity. Overallocation can lead to system instability or degrade the performance of other applications running on the host machine.

Optimizing Synced Folders

Synced folder issues can also contribute to performance degradation, especially when working with a large number of files or when frequent read/write operations are required. Vagrant offers several synced folder types, each with its own set of performance characteristics. For optimal performance, consider using the rsync or NFS synced folder types, which generally offer improved synchronization speeds compared to the default vboxsf option.

Configuring an NFS synced folder can be accomplished as follows:

```
1    config.vm.synced_folder ".", "/vagrant", type: "nfs"
```

Note that NFS may require additional setup on the host machine and is not supported on all operating systems, making it essential to validate compatibility before implementation.

Leveraging Lightweight Base Boxes

The choice of base box plays a significant role in Vagrant's performance. Opting for a lightweight, minimalistic base box can lead to faster boot times and more responsive development environments. It is advisable to select a base box that closely matches the production environment while minimizing unnecessary services or applications that can consume system resources.

251

Managing Provider-Specific Settings

When using providers like VirtualBox or VMware, accessing provider-specific settings to optimize performance can yield substantial improvements. For instance, enabling features such as hardware virtualization extensions can enhance the speed of virtual machines:

```
1  config.vm.provider "virtualbox" do |v|
2    v.customize ["modifyvm", :id, "--vtxvpid", "on"]
3  end
```

Such settings, however, should be applied with caution and tested thoroughly, as they might not be suitable for all development environments or host systems.

Identifying and resolving performance issues in Vagrant environments requires a comprehensive understanding of both Vagrant's configuration possibilities and the host system's resource constraints. By carefully analyzing resource allocation, optimizing synced folder usage, selecting appropriate base boxes, and adjusting provider-specific settings, developers can significantly enhance the performance of their Vagrant environments, leading to a more efficient and productive development workflow.

9.9 Dealing with Compatibility and Versioning Problems

One of the more complex issues a developer might encounter when using Vagrant centers on compatibility and versioning problems. Vagrant operates in conjunction with a variety of software, including host operating systems, guest operating systems, provisioners like Ansible, Chef, or Puppet, and virtualization providers such as VirtualBox, VMware, or Hyper-V. Compatibility issues can emerge between any of these components and Vagrant itself, potentially leading to challenging debugging scenarios.

Identifying Compatibility Issues

To efficiently resolve compatibility and versioning problems, the first step is identifying the precise nature of the issue. The error messages provided by Vagrant can often offer significant clues. These messages may indicate if a specific version of a dependency is required or if there is a known incompatibility with the current configuration.

```
1  $ vagrant up
2  There was an error while executing `VBoxManage`, a CLI used by Vagrant
3  for controlling VirtualBox. The command and stderr are shown below.
4  Command: ["startvm", "12345678-1234-1234-1234-123456789abc", "--type", "headless
       "]
5  Stderr: VBoxManage.exe: error: The virtual machine 'my_vagrant_vm' has
       terminated unexpectedly during startup with exit code 1 (0x1)
```

Here, the error output points towards an issue with VirtualBox. Investigating the compatibility between the Vagrant version in use and the installed version of VirtualBox is a recommended next step.

Resolving Version Conflicts

Once a compatibility or versioning issue has been identified, resolving it typically involves one of the following actions:

- Upgrading Vagrant or the conflicting software component to the latest version. However, this approach requires verifying that the upgrade does not introduce new compatibility issues with other parts of the development environment.

- Downgrading Vagrant or the conflicting component to a version known to be compatible. This might be a necessary step when working on projects that require specific software versions.

- Consulting the official Vagrant documentation or the documentation of the third-party software for notes on compatibility and any recommended workarounds.

Performing these steps can help overcome compatibility and versioning problems, but there are cases where manual adjustments to the Vagrantfile or other configuration files may be required. For example, adjusting the configuration to specify the use of an alternative provider or a different version of a provisioner can offer a solution.

Example: Specifying a Provider Version

In situations where the latest version of a provider such as VirtualBox introduces compatibility issues, specifying an earlier version of the provider within the Vagrantfile can offer a workaround. Consider the following code snippet:

```
1  Vagrant.configure("2") do |config|
2    config.vm.box = "ubuntu/xenial64"
3
4    config.vm.provider "virtualbox" do |v|
5      v.version = "5.2"
6    end
7  end
```

This configuration instructs Vagrant to use VirtualBox version 5.2, thereby avoiding issues associated with newer versions.

Prevention Strategies

To minimize encountering compatibility and versioning issues in the future, consider incorporating the following best practices into your workflow:

- Regularly check for updates from Vagrant, virtualization providers, and provisioners, but only apply these updates after confirming compatibility with the rest of your development environment.

- Utilize version control for your Vagrantfiles and other configuration scripts, allowing you to easily revert to earlier, compatible configurations if issues arise after an update.

- Leverage Vagrant's built-in support for specifying versions of boxes, providers, and plugins within the Vagrantfile to ensure consistent environments across multiple development machines.

By implementing these strategies, developers can significantly reduce the frequency and impact of compatibility and versioning problems, leading to a more stable and predictable development environment using Vagrant.

9.10 Advanced Debugging Techniques

Advanced debugging techniques go beyond the routine examination of logs or straightforward checking of configurations. They often involve a deeper understanding of Vagrant's interaction with both the host system and the guest machines. These techniques are particularly useful when standard troubleshooting steps fail to resolve the issue.

Interactive Debugging with Pry

One powerful tool for debugging provisioning scripts in Vagrant environments is Pry. Pry is a runtime developer console and IRB alternative for Ruby, which Vagrant is built upon. To use Pry for debugging your provisioning scripts, insert the following line at the point where you want to start your interactive debug session:

```
1  require 'pry'; binding.pry
```

This line temporarily halts the provisioning process and opens an interactive Ruby session in your terminal. Here, you can inspect variables, evaluate Ruby expressions, and step through code execution in real-time.

Analyzing Network Traffic with Wireshark

Networking issues can be particularly vexing to debug due to their often non-obvious nature. Tools like Wireshark, a network protocol analyzer, can be invaluable in understanding the data flow between your host machine, the virtual machine, and the wider network. To utilize Wireshark for debugging Vagrant networking issues, capture traffic on the virtual network interface connected to your Vagrant machine. This allows you to see the packets being transmitted and received, which can be essential in diagnosing problems like failed API calls, DNS issues, or incorrect firewall configurations.

Employing strace for System Calls Monitoring

The `strace` tool is indispensable when debugging issues at the system call level—particularly within Linux-based virtual machines. It monitors and displays system calls made by a process and the signals it receives. By attaching `strace` to a running process inside your Vagrant machine, you can obtain detailed information about file interactions, network operations, and other system-level events. This is especially helpful for uncovering hidden errors or identifying why a particular operation is failing.

Use the following command to attach `strace` to a running process by its PID:

```
1   strace -p <PID>
```

Where `<PID>` is replaced with the process identifier of the target process.

Leveraging Vagrant's Built-in Support for Debugging

Remember that Vagrant itself offers a `--debug` flag that can be appended to most commands to output extensive debugging information to the terminal. This information includes detailed logs of Vagrant's operations, interactions with virtualization providers (such as VirtualBox or VMware), and network configurations.

Analyzing this output can reveal subtle issues in how Vagrant interprets your Vagrantfile or interacts with external environments.

Example command to run Vagrant with debug mode enabled:

```
vagrant up --debug
```

Advanced debugging techniques require a combination of understanding Vagrant's underlying mechanisms, leveraging external tools for deep inspection, and occasional modifications to provisioning scripts or the Vagrantfile. With the methods outlined above, developers can diagnose and resolve even the most obscure issues within their Vagrant environments.

9.11 Community Support and Resources for Troubleshooting

Vagrant, akin to many open-source projects, benefits from a robust and active community. This community, composed of users ranging from beginners to advanced developers, provides a rich source of support and resources for troubleshooting and knowledge exchange. Herein, we will discuss the different avenues through which you can engage with the Vagrant community and external resources to resolve issues, with an emphasis on leveraging community wisdom for troubleshooting.

Online Forums and Question Boards

One primary resource are online forums and question boards, such as Stack Overflow and the Vagrant GitHub issues page. These platforms enable users to post specific issues or errors encountered while working with Vagrant and receive feedback and solutions from other community members. To effectively utilize these resources, there are several best practices one should follow:

- Provide a clear and concise description of the problem, includ-

257

ing the specific Vagrant version and host operating system.

- Include relevant portions of the `Vagrantfile` or error logs, enclosing them within `lstlisting` blocks to maintain readability.

- Before posting a new question, search the forum or issue tracker to see if the problem has already been discussed and potentially resolved.

- Show appreciation to community members who offer their help by upvoting or accepting their answers, where applicable.

Vagrant Documentation

Vagrant's official documentation should not be overlooked. Structured to cover a broad range of topics, from getting started guides to advanced features, the documentation is often the first place to check for solutions. The troubleshooting section within the documentation provides insights into common problems and their respective solutions.

IRC and Slack Channels

Real-time communication platforms like IRC and Slack host Vagrant channels where users can seek immediate help from others. These platforms are especially valuable for dynamic problem-solving and when seeking advice on best practices. Here are a few guidelines for engaging with community members on these channels:

- Introduce your problem succinctly, providing context and what you have attempted so far to resolve the issue.

- Be patient after posting a question; community members are volunteering their time and may not respond immediately.

- Contribute to discussions when you have insights or solutions to offer, fostering a positive cycle of community support.

Blogs and Tutorials

Many experienced Vagrant users share their knowledge through blogs and tutorials. These resources can prove invaluable for understanding both fundamental concepts and intricate details of Vagrant's functionality. They often include step-by-step guides, best practices, and workarounds for known issues. Employing search engines with specific keywords related to your problem can unearth related blog posts and tutorials.

Workshops and Meetups

Participating in workshops and meetups, whether virtual or in-person, offers opportunities for direct interaction with seasoned Vagrant users and developers. These events often feature sessions dedicated to troubleshooting and best practices, providing a platform for real-time discussion and networking.

In summary, the Vagrant community is a cornerstone of support for users navigating troubleshooting and debugging challenges. By engaging with online forums, leveraging official documentation, participating in real-time chats, exploring blogs and tutorials, and joining workshops and meetups, users can tap into a wealth of knowledge and experience. This collaborative approach not only aids in resolving specific issues but also contributes to continuous learning and proficiency in Vagrant.

9.12   Best Practices for Preventing Common Issues

To maintain an efficient workflow and minimize the likelihood of encountering common issues when using Vagrant, adopting a set of best practices is essential. These guidelines aim not just to avert potential problems but also to streamline the development process, ensuring that projects progress smoothly without unnecessary interruptions.

- **Regularly Update Vagrant and Providers:** Ensuring that Vagrant and its providers (e.g., VirtualBox, VMware) are kept up to date is crucial. Developers should routinely check for and apply updates, which often include bug fixes, security patches, and performance improvements.

```
1   # Check for Vagrant updates
2   vagrant version
3
4   # Update Vagrant
5   vagrant box update
```

This practice helps in avoiding compatibility issues and ensures access to the latest features and improvements.

- **Version Control for Vagrantfiles:** Employing version control systems like Git for `Vagrantfiles` and other configuration scripts ensures that changes are tracked, facilitating easy rollback to previous states in case of errors.

```
1   # Add Vagrantfile to Git
2   git add Vagrantfile
3   git commit -m "Add initial Vagrant configuration"
```

This approach provides a safety net, allowing developers to experiment with configurations in a controlled manner.

- **Utilize Provisioning Scripts Wisely:** Provisioning scripts automate the setup of the virtual environment, but they also introduce a layer of complexity. To avoid errors:

    - Use idempotent scripts that can run multiple times without causing issues.
    - Test scripts independently of Vagrant to ensure they perform as expected.
    - Keep scripts concise and document them thoroughly.

- **Consistent Networking Configuration:** Networking issues are among the most common problems faced when using Vagrant. Maintaining consistency in networking configurations across projects helps in reducing these issues.

    Configuring a private network:

```
config.vm.network "private_network", ip: "192.168.33.10"
```

Such practices make diagnosing and troubleshooting network-ing problems more manageable.

- **Allocate Sufficient Resources:** Allocating inadequate resources (such as memory and CPU) to the virtual machine can lead to performance issues. It's vital to:

  - Assess the resource demands of your development environment.
  - Allocate resources generously to avoid bottlenecks.

- **Employ Synced Folders Sparingly:** While synced folders are a compelling feature for file synchronization between the host and the guest machine, overuse or misconfiguration can lead to issues. Optimize their use by:

  - Limiting the number of synced folders.
  - Explicitly defining synced folders in the Vagrantfile to prevent unexpected behavior.

- **Stay Informed of Best Practices:** The development landscape is constantly evolving, and so are best practices. Regularly engaging with the Vagrant community through forums, official documentation, and tutorials can provide insights into new approaches and prevent potential pitfalls.

Incorporating these best practices into the development workflow significantly reduces the likelihood of encountering common issues with Vagrant. It fosters an environment where developers can focus more on the development itself rather than on resolving preventable errors.

Chapter 10

Integrating Vagrant with Development Workflows

Integrating Vagrant with Development Workflows exemplifies how Vagrant can be seamlessly incorporated into various stages of software development, from coding and testing to deployment. By aligning Vagrant's capabilities with version control systems, continuous integration/continuous deployment pipelines, and other development tools, teams can create a cohesive and automated process that ensures consistency across environments. This integration facilitates not only the development and testing of applications in environments that mimic production but also enhances collaboration among team members by using shared configurations. This chapter highlights strategies for embedding Vagrant into existing development workflows, discusses best practices for achieving automation and efficiency, and explores the benefits of a unified approach to managing development environments.

10.1 The Role of Vagrant in Modern Development Workflows

In this section we will discuss the crucial role that Vagrant plays in modern development workflows. Vagrant, a tool designed for building and managing virtual machine environments in a single workflow, provides a lightweight, reproducible, and portable development environment. This capability is invaluable in modern software development, where consistency across environments is a pivotal concern.

The adoption of Vagrant in development workflows offers several significant advantages:

- *Consistency*: Vagrant ensures that every member of the development team works in an environment that mirrors the production setting, thereby dramatically reducing the "it works on my machine" syndrome.

- *Efficiency*: By automating the provisioning of development environments, Vagrant saves developers time that would otherwise be spent setting up and troubleshooting individual environments.

- *Version Control for Environments*: With the capability to define environments as code via its Vagrantfiles, Vagrant allows the environmental configurations to be version-controlled and easily shared among team members, further enhancing consistency and collaboration.

- *Flexibility*: Vagrant supports multiple providers such as VirtualBox, VMware, AWS, and more, enabling developers to replicate production environments more accurately or leverage cloud resources efficiently.

Let's delve into a practical example that demonstrates the straightforwardness of initializing a new Vagrant environment. The following commands illustrate the process from creation to access:

```
1   # Initialize a new Vagrant environment
2   vagrant init hashicorp/bionic64
3
4   # Start the virtual machine
5   vagrant up
6
7   # SSH into the virtual machine
8   vagrant ssh
```

Upon executing the vagrant up command, Vagrant begins the process of creating and configuring the virtual machine based on the settings defined in the Vagrantfile. This process is repeatable, ensuring that every team member can create an identical development environment with minimal effort.

The integration of Vagrant with provisioning tools like Ansible, Chef, or Puppet further streamlines the process of environment setup. These tools can automate the installation and configuration of software within the Vagrant-managed virtual machines. An example of provisioning a web server using a shell script within the Vagrantfile is shown below:

```
1   Vagrant.configure("2") do |config|
2     config.vm.box = "hashicorp/bionic64"
3     config.vm.provision :shell, inline: <<-SHELL
4       apt-get update
5       apt-get install -y apache2
6     SHELL
7   end
```

The significance of Vagrant in modern development workflows is further exemplified by its role in facilitating the adoption of microservices architecture. By enabling developers to effortlessly manage and interact with multiple services running in separate environments, Vagrant acts as a catalyst for exploring and adopting architectural shifts that demand isolated environments for individual components of the application.

In essence, Vagrant lies at the heart of modern software development, owing to its capacity to bridge the gap between local development environments and production configurations. This ensures that software is developed, tested, and deployed in a manner that is both efficient and reliable, thereby emphasizing the role of Vagrant as an in-

266   CHAPTER 10.   INTEGRATING VAGRANT WITH DEVELOPMENT WORKFLOWS

dispensable tool in the arsenal of modern developers.

10.2   Integrating   Vagrant   with   Version Control Systems

Integrating Vagrant with version control systems (VCS) represents a significant step towards achieving an effective and streamlined development workflow. The essence of this integration lies in the ability to maintain the Vagrant configuration files, such as `Vagrantfile`, within the same version control repository as the application code. This approach ensures that any changes to the development environment can be tracked, rolled back, or shared among team members just as easily as application code changes.

- The first step in this integration process involves creating a `Vagrantfile` at the root of the application's repository. This file contains all necessary configuration details for Vagrant to provision and manage the virtual development environments.

- It is advisable to include a `.gitignore` or similar version control ignore file to exclude temporary files generated by Vagrant (e.g., `.vagrant/`), which do not need to be shared or versioned.

- Documenting the purpose and usage of each part of the `Vagrantfile` within the repository's README or similar documentation is important for enhancing team collaboration and understanding.

```
1  # Example of a simple Vagrantfile
2  Vagrant.configure("2") do |config|
3    config.vm.box = "hashicorp/bionic64"
4    config.vm.network "private_network", type: "dhcp"
5  end
```

When this `Vagrantfile` is committed to a VCS, any team member who clones the repository will be able to instantiate an identical development environment by simply executing `vagrant up`.

Version Control Considerations for Vagrant Environments

Maintaining a clean and maintainable Vagrantfile becomes crucial as it directly impacts the ease of use and clarity for all team members. Several best practices include:

- Minimize customization in individual development environments to ensure consistency across all team members' environments.

- Use version control branching strategies to manage different configurations of Vagrant environments, similar to how application feature branches are managed.

- Consider the use of Vagrant plugins to integrate more deeply with version control systems, enhancing the automation and management capabilities of Vagrant environments.

Integration with CI/CD pipelines can be achieved by ensuring the build and test scripts reference the version-controlled `Vagrantfile`, enabling automatic provisioning of testing environments that mimic the development environment closely.

Collaborating with Shared Vagrant Boxes

To further enhance collaboration and environment consistency, teams can create custom Vagrant boxes that include preconfigured settings, software, and dependencies necessary for the application development. These custom boxes can be versioned and stored in a shared location accessible to all team members, ensuring that every member starts with the same base environment.

When updating these custom boxes, it's important to version the boxes appropriately and update the `Vagrantfile` in the version control system to reference the new box version, ensuring all team members are using the most up-to-date environment.

```
==> default: Importing base box 'hashicorp/bionic64'...
```

Security Implications

While integrating Vagrant with VCS, security aspects should not be overlooked. Sensitive information, such as API keys or credentials, must never be stored in the `Vagrantfile` or any script files versioned in VCS. Instead, utilize environment variables or encrypted secrets management services to handle sensitive data securely.

In summary, the integration of Vagrant with version control systems offers a multitude of benefits for development teams, including environment consistency, ease of collaboration, and the ability to track and revert environmental changes with the same ease as application code. Following best practices for Vagrantfile management and security can significantly enhance the development workflow, making it more efficient and robust.

10.3 Using   Vagrant   in   Continuous Integration/Continuous   Deployment Pipelines

Continuous Integration (CI) and Continuous Deployment (CD) are vital components of modern development workflows, aiming to automate the process of integrating code changes and deploying applications. Introducing Vagrant into CI/CD pipelines can significantly enhance the consistency and reliability of builds and deployments by ensuring every team member works in a development environment that mirrors the production environment as closely as possible.

To integrate Vagrant into CI/CD pipelines effectively, it is essential to understand the process flow and the role Vagrant plays in each stage.   Vagrant facilitates the creation and configuration of lightweight, reproducible, and portable development environments, making it an invaluable tool for CI/CD practices.

- **Source Code Repository Integration**: The first step involves integrating Vagrant configurations with the source code repository. This ensures that any changes to the development environment are version-controlled alongside the application code. For example, a Vagrantfile could be included at the root of the repository, specifying the required virtual machine (VM) configurations and provisioning scripts.

```
1   Vagrant.configure("2") do |config|
2     config.vm.box = "ubuntu/bionic64"
3     config.vm.provision :shell, path: "bootstrap.sh"
4   end
```

- **Automating Environment Setup in CI Server**: When a CI server (such as Jenkins, Travis CI, or CircleCI) detects a new commit, it can use Vagrant to spin up a VM based on the configurations stored in the Vagrantfile. This VM serves as the base environment for running further integration tests or builds.

```
1   # Example CI pipeline script
2   - echo "Initializing Vagrant environment..."
3   - vagrant up
4   - echo "Environment ready. Running tests..."
```

- **Running Tests**: With the development environment set up, the pipeline proceeds to run automated tests. These tests are executed within the Vagrant-provisioned environment, ensuring they run under conditions that mimic the production environment as closely as possible.

```
Test Suite: Application Tests
Tests run: 10, Failures: 0, Errors: 0, Skipped: 0
```

- **Deployment**: If tests pass, the CI server can trigger a deployment script that applies the necessary changes to the production environment. Vagrant can also assist in staging environments for pre-production deployments, ensuring that the application behaves as expected in an environment that mimics production.

- **Cleanup**: After tests are completed or a deployment is made, the CI server can shut down and destroy the Vagrant environment, freeing up resources until the next commit triggers the pipeline.

```
1    - echo "Tests and deployment completed. Cleaning up..."
2    - vagrant destroy -f
```

Integrating Vagrant into CI/CD pipelines offers several advantages, such as ensuring consistency across development, testing, and production environments, facilitating early detection of potential deployment issues, and streamlining the onboarding process for new team members by providing them with quickly provisionable development environments. However, it is also essential to be mindful of potential challenges such as increased build times due to environment provisioning and the need for robust hardware resources on the CI server to handle multiple VMs efficiently.

Leveraging Vagrant within CI/CD pipelines is a powerful strategy to reinforce the principles of continuous integration and deployment. By automating the creation and management of development environments, development teams can focus more on feature development and less on environment discrepancies, leading to more reliable and frequent releases.

10.4   Collaboration Using Shared Vagrant Environments

Collaboration using shared Vagrant environments requires a well-structured approach to ensure that all team members are operating within the same development conditions. This harmonization is critical for minimizing "it works on my machine" scenarios, increasing productivity, and ensuring that all development activities are aligned with the project's requirements. The core of this strategy involves creating a Vagrant configuration file, typically 'Vagrantfile', which defines the properties of the development environment in a way that can be uniformly replicated across different machines.

To begin with, it is essential to understand the constituents of a 'Vagrantfile'. At its core, the file specifies the base image to use, network configurations, shared folders, and provisioning scripts.

```
1  Vagrant.configure("2") do |config|
2    config.vm.box = "ubuntu/bionic64"
3    config.vm.network "private_network", ip: "192.168.33.10"
4    config.vm.synced_folder "./data", "/vagrant_data"
5    config.vm.provision "shell", inline: <<-SHELL
6      apt-get update
7      apt-get install -y apache2
8    SHELL
9  end
```

This example demonstrates a basic setup where an Ubuntu 18.04 LTS box is used. The machine is assigned a private network IP, a folder from the host is shared with the guest, and a provisioning script that installs Apache2 is executed.

When sharing Vagrant environments for collaboration, version control systems (VCS) like Git are invaluable. The 'Vagrantfile' and any associated provisioning scripts or configuration files should be committed to a repository. This approach allows any team member to clone the repository and, with Vagrant installed, execute 'vagrant up' to replicate the development environment locally.

```
$ vagrant up
Bringing machine 'default' up with 'virtualbox' provider...
==> default: Importing base box 'ubuntu/bionic64'...
```

One key factor in collaboration is ensuring that every team member is employing the same version of Vagrant and the underlying provider, such as VirtualBox or VMware. This consistency can be enforced through the use of a '.vagrantversion' file that specifies the required versions, and a simple shell script can be created to check these versions before 'vagrant up' is run.

In addition to sharing environments, it is important to keep the base images (boxes) up to date. Vagrant can check for updates automatically or you can manually update the boxes to ensure that everyone is using the latest versions with critical security and performance updates.

```
1  vagrant box update
```

For larger teams or projects, leveraging Vagrant Cloud can simplify box distribution. Custom boxes can be created, versioned, and hosted in Vagrant Cloud, making it straightforward for team members to access and use the exact same environment.

- Ensures environment consistency across different systems

- Simplifies the process of setting up development environments

- Facilitates the sharing of environments and their automated provisioning

- Enables version control of development environments

Collaboration using shared Vagrant environments is a powerful strategy for ensuring that all team members work in an identical setup, thus mitigating discrepancies in development and testing. By leveraging Vagrant's capabilities in combination with version control systems and adherence to version consistency, teams can significantly enhance their development workflows, improve productivity, and reduce the time spent on environment-related issues.

10.5   Leveraging Vagrant with Cloud Services

Leveraging Vagrant with cloud services unlocks a plethora of opportunities for development teams to scale their applications and infrastructure while obtaining the benefits of cloud computing, such as flexibility, scalability, and high availability. When integrated with cloud services, Vagrant enables developers to manage infrastructure across various cloud platforms using a consistent workflow, reducing the complexity inherent in using multiple providers and technologies. This section will discuss strategies for integrating Vagrant with cloud services and the advantages this brings to development workflows.

Vagrant, primarily known for its capacity to create and manage virtual machine (VM) environments, significantly simplifies the process of configuring these environments to mirror production settings. However, modern development often requires more than just VMs, extending into the realm of cloud computing for resources such as storage, databases, and application services. Here, we explore how to extend Vagrant environments into the cloud, utilizing providers like AWS, Azure, and Google Cloud Platform.

```
1   Vagrant.configure("2") do |config|
2     config.vm.provider :aws do |aws, override|
3       aws.access_key_id = "YOUR_ACCESS_KEY"
4       aws.secret_access_key = "YOUR_SECRET_KEY"
5       aws.instance_type = "t2.micro"
6       aws.region = "us-east-1"
7       aws.ami = "ami-abcdefgh"
8       override.ssh.username = "ubuntu"
9     end
10  end
```

The code snippet above illustrates the basic configuration for provisioning an AWS EC2 instance using Vagrant. This lightweight and easily readable DSL (Domain-Specific Language) allows developers to manage cloud instances with the same ease as managing local VMs. The configuration specifies the AWS access key, secret key, desired instance type, region, and Amazon Machine Image (AMI) to use, along with the SSH username.

Integrating Vagrant with cloud services involves several key strategies:

- Utilizing provider-specific plugins to extend Vagrant's capability to manage resources in the cloud. These plugins are available for most major cloud providers, including AWS, Azure, and Google Cloud Platform.

- Leveraging Vagrant's provisioning capabilities to automate the setup of environments on cloud instances, which can include software installation, configuration, and the automation of deployment tasks.

- Employing Vagrant's multi-machine configurations to orchestrate the deployment of complex applications across multiple cloud instances, facilitating scenarios such as load-balancing and microservices architectures.

The integration of Vagrant with cloud services offers several advantages:

- **Consistency**: By using the same tooling and configuration approaches across different environments, teams can ensure consistency between development, staging, and production.

- **Portability**: Vagrant's abstraction over cloud services allows developers to migrate workloads across different cloud providers with minimal changes to configuration, promoting a higher degree of application portability.

- **Automation**: The automation of resource provisioning and environment configuration streamlines the development process, reducing manual intervention and potential for human error.

However, there are considerations teams must account for when integrating Vagrant with cloud services. These include understanding the cost implications of cloud resources, managing access and security keys, and ensuring compliance with data protection regulations. Moreover, teams should be prepared to tackle the complexities of networking and storage configuration in cloud environments, tasks that require thorough understanding of both Vagrant and the specific cloud provider's offerings.

Leveraging Vagrant with cloud services facilitates not only the orchestration of VM environments but also the comprehensive management of cloud resources. This approach aids in achieving a streamlined, consistent, and automated workflow, essential for modern development practices.

10.6   Vagrant in a DevOps Context

In the dynamically evolving landscape of software development, the DevOps philosophy aims to bridge the gap between development (Dev) and operations (Ops) teams, fostering a culture of collaborative and seamless workflow. The incorporation of

Vagrant within this context serves as a catalyst, enhancing both productivity and operational efficiency. This section will dissect the role of Vagrant in DevOps, elucidating on its contributions to environment consistency, automation, and the overall acceleration of the delivery process.

Vagrant's pivotal role in DevOps stems from its ability to create lightweight, reproducible, and portable development environments. These environments can be configured to closely mirror production settings, thereby minimizing the "it works on my machine" syndrome—a common cause of friction within teams. By enabling developers to work in a standardized environment, Vagrant significantly reduces the time spent on troubleshooting environmental discrepancies, paving the way for a more streamlined development process.

The alignment of Vagrant with DevOps practices can be observed through several key functionalities:

- *Configuration as Code (CaC)*: Vagrant leverages Vagrantfiles to define and configure development environments in code, which can be version-controlled. This aligns with the CaC principle, promoting environment consistency, traceability, and ease of automation.

- *Automation*: With Vagrant, the provisioning of environments can be automated using various provisioners such as Shell scripts, Ansible, Chef, or Puppet. This automation capability is critical in DevOps, as it contributes to the rapid iteration and deployment cycles, ensuring that the environments are set up and torn down without manual intervention.

- *Integration with CI/CD Pipelines*: Vagrant environments can be integrated into Continuous Integration and Continuous Deployment (CI/CD) pipelines. This allows for code and environment changes to be automatically tested in a consistent manner, further enhancing the delivery speed and reliability.

To illustrate Vagrant's integration into a CI/CD pipeline, consider the following scenario where a Vagrant box is used for running automated tests:

```
1   # Example of defining a Vagrant environment for CI/CD testing
2   Vagrant.configure("2") do |config|
3     config.vm.box = "hashicorp/bionic64"
4     config.vm.provision "shell", inline: <<-SHELL
5       echo "Install dependencies..."
6       apt-get update && apt-get install -y nginx
7       echo "Dependencies installed."
8     SHELL
9     # Additional configuration for network, synced folders, etc.
10  end
```

Once defined, this environment can be instantiated and utilized in the CI/CD pipeline to ensure that the application behaves as expected in a controlled setting that mimics the production environment.

Vagrant's versatility extends beyond individual developer environments, facilitating collaborations within teams and across departments. This collaborative aspect is crucial in DevOps, promoting a culture of shared responsibility and continuous feedback. By sharing Vagrant environments, teams can effortlessly replicate issues, share advancements, and maintain consistency throughout the software development lifecycle (SDLC).

Vagrant's integration into DevOps practices is not merely advantageous but transformative. It underpins the principles of environment consistency, automation, and collaboration—cornerstones of the DevOps philosophy. Through the strategic employment of Vagrant, organizations can achieve not only a harmonized Dev and Ops workflow but also a substantial enhancement in the speed and reliability of their software delivery processes.

10.7   Automating Development Environment Provisioning

Automating the provisioning of development environments through Vagrant is a crucial step in reducing the time and effort developers must invest in setting up consistent, reproducible environments for their projects. This process involves creating a Vagrantfile that contains all necessary configuration to automatically set up the environment upon the initial invocation of Vagrant. Automation not only streamlines the setup process but also ensures that all team members are working within the same environment, thus minimizing the "it works on my machine" syndrome and improving overall productivity and collaboration.

At the foundation of this automation is the Vagrantfile, a Ruby-based configuration file leveraged by Vagrant to provision and manage virtual environments. The versatility of the Vagrantfile allows for the specification of various aspects of the development environment, including the base box (operating system), network configurations, synced folders, and crucially, the automation of environment setup through the use of shell scripts or configuration management tools such as Puppet, Chef, or Ansible.

```
1   # Example Vagrantfile Configuration
2   Vagrant.configure("2") do |config|
3     config.vm.box = "ubuntu/bionic64"
4
5     # Network Configuration
6     config.vm.network "private_network", type: "dhcp"
7
8     # Synced Folder
9     config.vm.synced_folder "./host_folder", "/vm_folder"
10
11    # Provisioning Script
12    config.vm.provision "shell", inline: <<-SHELL
13      apt-get update
14      apt-get install -y apache2
15    SHELL
16  end
```

The provisioning script within the Vagrantfile is a potent means of automating the setup of the virtual environment. Here, developers can specify commands to install software, create configurations,

277

and perform other tasks needed to prepare the environment for development. When a team member runs vagrant up, Vagrant processes this file, creating a virtual machine that matches the specifications laid out, including the execution of the provisioning script, which configures the VM according to the project's needs.

For more complex environments, or when more repeatability across multiple projects is needed, leveraging external configuration management tools becomes invaluable. Instead of shell scripts, Vagrant can be configured to use tools such as Ansible, allowing for the application of detailed, idempotent configuration strategies that can be version controlled and shared among team members.

```
# Using Ansible for provisioning
Vagrant.configure("2") do |config|
  config.vm.box = "ubuntu/bionic64"

  # Ansible Provisioning
  config.vm.provision "ansible" do |ansible|
    ansible.playbook = "playbook.yml"
  end
end
```

Through the example above, an Ansible playbook is specified, which Vagrant executes during the provisioning process. This playbook contains the automation logic in YAML format, detailing tasks such as software installations and configuration changes. The advantage here is the readability and simplicity of YAML combined with the powerful automation capabilities of Ansible, creating a more maintainable and scalable approach to environment provisioning.

Automating the provisioning of development environments using Vagrant represents a significant stride towards efficient and consistent development workflows. By encapsulating environment configurations into a Vagrantfile, and optionally integrating with configuration management tools, teams can quickly spin up identical development environments, ensuring that all members are working under the same conditions and drastically reducing setup time and potential discrepancies between environments. This process fosters collaboration, enhances productivity, and ultimately leads to a more streamlined development lifecycle.

10.8 Managing   Dependencies   and Versioning in Team Environments

Managing dependencies and versioning in team environments is a critical aspect that requires attentive strategy and execution to prevent conflicts and maintain a seamless workflow. The core of this task in a Vagrant-integrated development workflow lies in the appropriate management of Vagrant boxes, provisioning scripts, and version control practices which ensure that all team members are working within identical development conditions.

Version Control for Vagrant Files: It is essential to maintain `Vagrantfile` and provisioning scripts within a version control system (VCS). This practice ensures that changes to the development environment are tracked, reasoned about, and shared among team members effectively. Consider including the following within a VCS:

- `Vagrantfile` – This includes the base box configuration, network settings, synced folders, and provider-specific configurations.

- Provisioning scripts – Scripts for software installation and configuration within the Vagrant box, such as shell scripts, Ansible playbooks, or Puppet manifests.

- Environment-specific configuration files – These files may include database configuration, application environment variables, or any other configuration files required for the application to run.

Here is a simple example of how to use Git to track changes to a `Vagrantfile`:

```
1  git add Vagrantfile
2  git commit -m "Updated Vagrantfile to include new synced folder settings"
3  git push origin master
```

Using Version Constraints for Boxes: It is recommended to specify version constraints for Vagrant boxes used in projects. This ensures that all team members are using the same version of the box, preventing discrepancies between environments. In the `Vagrantfile`, specify the box version as follows:

```
1   config.vm.box = "hashicorp/precise64"
2   config.vm.box_version = "~> 1.1.0"
```

This utilizes semantic versioning to allow updates that do not include breaking changes. The ' >' operator is used to accept patch-level changes within a specified minor version.

Dependency Management Tools: Leveraging dependency management tools such as 'Bundler' for Ruby or 'npm' for Node.js is pivotal in ensuring that all dependencies within the Vagrant environment are precisely versioned. This practice guarantees that the installation of dependencies is reproducible across all team members' environments.

For example, using 'Bundler' with a 'Gemfile' to manage Ruby dependencies can be integrated into the provisioning process as follows:

```
1   # In the provisioning script
2   gem install bundler
3   cd /vagrant/my_project
4   bundle install
```

The 'Gemfile' should be version-controlled, ensuring that all team members install the exact versions of the gems specified.

Versioning Strategies: Adopting a clear versioning strategy for the project itself is crucial. Semantic versioning (SemVer) is a widely accepted standard that can be applied. SemVer uses a three-part number scheme (MAJOR.MINOR.PATCH) and governs how versions should be incremented based on the nature of changes (e.g., bug fixes, new features, breaking changes).

Continuous Integration: Integrating Vagrant environments with continuous integration (CI) pipelines can help in automatically testing the impact of environment changes. CI can be configured to rebuild the Vagrant environment using the latest configurations and verify that the application behaves as expected. This reinforces the stability and consistency of the development environment across different stages of the development workflow.

Managing dependencies and versioning in team environments with Vagrant requires a comprehensive strategy that encompasses version control of environment configurations, precise dependency management, thoughtful versioning of the project, and integration with continuous integration pipelines. By adhering to these practices, teams can achieve a high level of consistency and efficiency in their development workflows, mitigating environment-related discrepancies and focusing on delivering high-quality software.

10.9   Scaling Vagrant Environments for Large Projects

Scaling Vagrant environments to accommodate large projects is an essential step for teams looking to maintain efficiency and consistency as they grow. Larger projects often involve more complex configurations, a greater number of environments, and increased demands on resources. Therefore, thoughtful approaches to scaling are required to ensure that the potential benefits of using Vagrant are not outweighed by the complexities introduced by a project's scale.

One primary consideration when scaling Vagrant environments is the management of Vagrantfiles. A Vagrantfile defines the configuration of a Vagrant environment; for large projects, managing multiple Vagrantfiles strategically is vital. The use of a hierarchical Vagrantfile structure allows for shared configurations at a higher level with the ability to override or extend these settings in child Vagrantfiles for specific environments. This approach promotes reuse and reduces duplication.

```
1   # Example of a parent Vagrantfile
2   Vagrant.configure("2") do |config|
3     config.vm.box = "generic/ubuntu1804"
4   end
5
6   # Child Vagrantfile in a subdirectory
7   Vagrant.configure("2") do |config|
```

```
8    config.vm.network "private_network", type: "dhcp"
9    end
```

Leveraging provisioning scripts is another effective technique for scaling. Provisioning scripts automate the setup of the development environment within the VM, installing necessary software, and configuring settings. For large projects, maintaining a library of reusable scripts for different parts of the environment can save considerable time and ensure consistency across team members' environments.

```
1    # Example provisioning script using Shell
2    config.vm.provision "shell", inline: <<-SHELL
3      apt-get update
4      apt-get install -y apache2
5    SHELL
```

When projects grow, the resource demands on developer machines can become a significant issue. Efficient resource utilization becomes critical. Vagrant allows for the configuration of each virtual machine's CPU and memory allocations, enabling teams to find a balance between performance and resource usage.

```
1    config.vm.provider "virtualbox" do |v|
2      v.memory = 1024
3      v.cpus = 2
4    end
```

To effectively scale Vagrant environments for large projects, integrating with cloud services becomes highly beneficial. Cloud providers, such as AWS, Azure, or Google Cloud, can host Vagrant environments, offloading the resources required from local machines and providing scalable infrastructure. Vagrant's plugin system supports integration with these cloud services, allowing environments to be deployed directly to the cloud.

```
1    # Example of specifying a provider for AWS
2    config.vm.provider :aws do |aws, override|
3      aws.access_key_id = "YOUR ACCESS KEY"
4      aws.secret_access_key = "YOUR SECRET KEY"
5      aws.instance_type = "t2.medium"
6    end
```

Another aspect that becomes increasingly important as projects scale is the efficient management of network configurations, especially when dealing with multiple environments that need to communicate with each other or with external services. Vagrant supports a range of network configurations including private networks, forwarded ports, and public networks, which can be tailored to match the needs of a large project.

For projects requiring simultaneous development on multiple related components, leveraging multi-machine Vagrant environments allows for defining configurations for different roles (e.g., web server, database server) within a single Vagrantfile. This facilitates a more integrated development process by simulating production-like multi-tier architectures.

```
Bringing machine 'web' up with 'virtualbox' provider...
Bringing machine 'db' up with 'virtualbox' provider...
```

Scaling Vagrant environments for large projects involves strategic management of Vagrantfiles, efficient provisioning, careful resource allocation, integration with cloud services, sophisticated network management, and the use of multi-machine setups. By addressing these areas, teams can extend the benefits of Vagrant throughout the lifecycle of large-scale projects, ensuring development environments are as consistent, efficient, and scalable as possible.

10.10   Monitoring and Maintaining Vagrant Environments

Monitoring and maintaining Vagrant environments is critical for ensuring that development workflows remain efficient, secure, and up-to-date. This involves regular checks on the health of the environments, updates to the base boxes, management of provisioning scripts, and ensuring security through up-to-date configurations and patches.

First, let's discuss the process of monitoring Vagrant environments. Monitoring involves observing the state and performance of Vagrant-based development environments. Key aspects include tracking resource usage such as CPU, memory, and disk space, as well as networking issues that might affect the connectivity between the host system and the Vagrant virtual machines (VMs).

```
CPU Usage: 75%
Memory Usage: 65%
Disk Space Remaining: 10GB
Network Connectivity: Stable
```

These metrics can be gathered using tools integrated into the host operating system or third-party monitoring solutions. It's essential to set up alerts for critical thresholds to avoid disruptions in the development process.

Maintaining Vagrant environments entails several practices aimed at ensuring the environments' longevity and reliability. This includes:

- Regularly updating the base boxes to benefit from the latest OS improvements and security patches.

- Keeping provisioning scripts, such as those written in Ansible, Chef, or Puppet, in sync with the application development needs.

- Managing dependencies within the Vagrant environments to prevent conflicts and ensure that all necessary libraries and packages are at their appropriate versions.

- Implementing security practices, including periodic audits, applying necessary patches, and securing network communication between the host and guest machines.

Updating base boxes is accomplished by issuing the following command, which should be performed periodically or as part of a scheduled task within the development ecosystem:

```
1  vagrant box update
```

This command checks for updates to the base box used by Vagrant environments and applies them if available. It's crucial to test the environments after updates to avoid disruptions.

Maintaining provisioning scripts involves reviewing and adjusting them according to the changing requirements of the development project. This includes adding or removing packages, adjusting configurations, or modifying scripts to integrate new tools or services.

Dependency management within Vagrant environments can be handled through configuration management tools or by specifying version constraints in provisioning scripts. Ensuring that all dependencies are correctly versioned and compatible is fundamental for maintaining environment stability.

Security practices include configuring firewalls within Vagrant environments, using encrypted communication channels, and keeping the guest operating systems and installed packages up-to-date with security patches. Regular security audits can identify vulnerabilities and help maintain secure development workflows.

$$\text{Security\_Score} = \text{Function}(\text{Updates\_Applied}, \text{Vulnerabilities\_Mitigated}, \text{Audits\_Passed}) \tag{10.1}$$

In summary, monitoring and maintaining Vagrant environments are integral parts of the development workflow. By implementing these practices, development teams can ensure that environments remain efficient, secure, and aligned with project requirements, thus facilitating a smoother transition from development to production.

10.11 Security Best Practices in Shared Development Workflows

In shared development workflows, maintaining a strong security posture is critical to protecting proprietary code, sensitive data, and system integrity. The integration of Vagrant environments into these workflows presents unique security challenges and requires adherence to best practices to ensure a secure development lifecycle.

Firstly, it's imperative to manage Vagrant box versions meticulously. A Vagrant box is a packaged Vagrant environment that can be distributed among team members. Boxes can contain a full operating system that might include outdated or vulnerable software components. To mitigate potential risks, teams should:

- Regularly check for updates on the base boxes from providers and ensure that the latest, most secure version is being used.

- Customize boxes with only the necessary packages and services to minimize the attack surface.

- Use boxes from trusted sources or, if possible, create custom boxes to have complete control over the box content.

Versioning and controlling box distribution through a version control system can further enhance security by ensuring that changes are tracked and that boxes can be audited for unauthorized modifications.

In addition, securing the Vagrantfile is of paramount importance. The Vagrantfile, which defines the configuration of Vagrant environments, can include sensitive information such as network configurations, synced folder paths, and provisioning scripts that may expose vulnerabilities if improperly configured. Best practices include:

```
1  # Encrypt sensitive data within the Vagrantfile
2  # Example: Use environment variables instead of hardcoding credentials
3  config.vm.provision "shell", inline: "export SECRET_KEY=#{ENV['SECRET_KEY']}"
```

It is also advisable to limit access to the Vagrantfile by storing it in a secure repository with restricted access controls. Reviews and audits of Vagrantfiles should be conducted regularly to ensure that configurations do not introduce security risks.

Utilizing Vagrant's networking features requires careful consideration to avoid inadvertently exposing the development environment to unauthorized access. Configuring private networks whenever possible is recommended, as it isolates the development environment from external networks. If a public network configuration is necessary, leveraging firewall rules to restrict inbound traffic is crucial. An example configuration to create a private network within Vagrant is as follows:

```
1  # Configure a private network
2  config.vm.network "private_network", type: "dhcp"
```

Another critical aspect of securing shared development workflows is the management of SSH keys used for accessing Vagrant environments. Shared keys or weak passphrase practices undermine security and can lead to unauthorized access. Best practices include:

- Generating individual SSH keys for each team member.

- Using strong passphrases for SSH keys.

- Rotating SSH keys periodically and revoking access for keys that are no longer in use.

Finally, integrating security testing tools and practices into the development process can help identify and mitigate vulnerabilities early. Tools such as static code analyzers, vulnerability scanners, and integration with CI/CD pipelines for automated security assessments can be valuable assets in upholding security standards.

A combination of diligent management of Vagrant components, secure configuration practices, and the integration of security testing into the development workflow constitutes a robust approach to maintaining security in shared development environments. By implementing these best practices, teams can leverage the benefits of Vagrant while minimizing security risks.

10.12   Transitioning from Development to Production with Vagrant

Transitioning from development to production environments represents a critical phase in the software development lifecycle. Vagrant, primarily utilized for creating and managing virtual development environments, also provides substantial benefits during this phase. This section explores strategies for leveraging Vagrant to ensure a smooth, error-free transition from development to production.

To begin, it's essential to understand the environment parity. Environment parity refers to maintaining consistency across development, staging, and production environments. This consistency is crucial for minimizing "works on my machine" problems, ensuring that software behaves the same way in production as it does in development.

- To achieve environment parity, ensure that the base boxes in Vagrant mirror the production environment as closely as possible. This includes the operating system, installed packages, system libraries, and configuration settings.

Next, we delve into the configuration management tools integration. Vagrant supports provisioning tools like Ansible, Chef, Puppet, and Salt, which can automate the process of configuring virtual machines. These tools can be used to apply the same configurations to both development and production environments, enhancing consistency.

```
1  # Example of using Vagrant with Ansible for provisioning
2  Vagrant.configure("2") do |config|
3    config.vm.provision "ansible" do |ansible|
4      ansible.playbook = "playbook.yml"
5    end
```

This snippet illustrates the ease with which one can integrate Ansible for provisioning in Vagrant, applying the same playbook used for development environments to configure production systems.

Version control systems play a pivotal role in this transition. It's advisable to version control not only application source code but also Vagrantfiles, provisioning scripts, and configuration management code. This practice ensures that any member of the team can replicate the environment, and changes can be tracked and audited.

Commit e3d5bc3 added new security patches to the production environment configuration.

The code output example indicates a commit message in version control, highlighting an update to the production environment configuration.

Another valuable strategy is the incorporation of continuous integration/continuous deployment (CI/CD) pipelines. Vagrant environments can be used within CI/CD pipelines to test the application in an environment that closely mimics the production setup before the actual deployment. This level of testing is beneficial for identifying environment-specific issues early.

Lastly, let's touch upon transitioning to production. While Vagrant is predominantly a tool for development environments, its role in transitioning to production involves the use of identical provisioning scripts and environment configurations. For actual deployment, tools like Docker can be used in conjunction with Vagrant to containerize applications, thereby facilitating deployment to production servers.

$$\text{Efficiency} = \frac{\text{Number of successful deployments}}{\text{Number of deployment attempts}} \qquad (10.2)$$

This equation underscores the importance of efficiency in deployment processes. A higher ratio reflects a streamlined, error-free transition from development to production, which can be achieved through the practices described here.

Transitioning from development to production with Vagrant involves maintaining environment parity, leveraging configuration management tools, adhering to version control best practices, incorporating CI/CD pipelines, and a careful approach to deployment. By adopting these strategies, teams can reduce discrepancies between environments, mitigate deployment risks, and ensure a smoother transition to production.

www.ingramcontent.com/pod-product-compliance
Lightning Source LLC
La Vergne TN
LVHW022337060326
832902LV00022B/4080